National Pr...
Derek Foster

"His (Derek Foster's) seductively simple approach... resonated with tens of thousands of Canadians who bought his bestselling books..." — *Globe and Mail*

"Thanks to a healthy stock portfolio, Derek Foster retired when he was 34 years old." — *Toronto Star*

"Thanks to a solid investment plan and a knack for picking the right stocks he (Derek Foster) was able to retire, mortgage-free, at the age of 34."

— *ROBTV (forerunner to BNN)*

"He's (Derek Foster) playing his very own game, which he's winning..." — *National Post*

"...— and he did it by turning the whole concept of what it means to save for retirement on its head."

— *Moneysense Magazine*

"While Warren Buffett is known as the Oracle of Omaha, investment whiz Derek Foster could be labelled the Wise Man of Wasaga Beach." — *Toronto Sun*

The Idiot Millionaire

YOU *Can* Become Wealthy!

Using this

"Idiot-Proof" Strategy

Derek Foster

FOSTER, UNDERHILL FINANCIAL PRESS

Copyright © 2011 by Derek Foster

Library and Archives Canada Cataloguing in Publication
Foster, Derek, 1970-
    The idiot millionaire, you can become wealthy! : using this list of idiot-proof stocks / Derek Foster.

ISBN 978-0-9736960-4-2

    1. Retirement income--Planning. 2. Investments. 3. Finance, Personal. I. Title.

HG179.F664 2010   332.024'014   C2010-906824-6

Published by
Foster, Underhill Financial Press
900 Greenbank Road, Suite 508
Ottawa, ON K2J 4P6
Canada
Phone toll free at: 1 888 686 STOP (1 888 686 7867)
or 613 823 2143
www.stopworking.ca

Page layout and print production: WeMakeBooks.ca
Printed and bound in Canada

LEGAL DISCLAIMER

This book is intended to show you a strategy that you might want to consider for investing.

However, you must realize that I am not a professional with regard to any of the information I've provided in this book. I am merely presenting a strategy that I feel might be of interest to you. I am not an expert in economic, legal, taxation, investing, realty, or any other financial or related matters. The examples I provide are just that—examples. These are intended for illustrative purposes only. They are not an indication of what rate of return or future amount of money you might have if you followed the specific examples. They are only presented to illustrate the general concepts. Before initiating any of the strategies outlined, seek the advice of a competent professional to help you.

The book is intended as a general guide and should not be viewed as the ultimate source for financial information.

Further research is needed and assistance must be sought from a qualified expert, before any action is taken by the reader. For further information, there is a recommended reading list at the back of this book. The information in this book might be incomplete, inaccurate, or out of date, so the reader should verify any of this information before acting on it.

For full disclosure, I must say that I (Derek Foster) own many of the securities mentioned in this book. The reader must also understand that any investing activity entails certain degrees of risk. Although lists of securities are presented in the book, the reader must understand that these securities do carry risk and should seek the advice from a qualified expert before acting upon any of the information.

Furthermore, this book might contain various errors, omissions, or mistakes of either a typographical nature or within the content itself. The reader must not rely on the accuracy of any of the information given, but should seek proper verification.

The author (Derek Foster) and the publisher (Foster Underhill Financial Press) shall have neither liability nor responsibility to any person or other legal entity with respect to any sort of loss or damage or perceived damage caused, or alleged to have been caused by the information provided in this book. By reading this, you fully accept these conditions. If for any reason, you do not with to be bound by any or all of the above conditions, you many simply return this book to the publisher for a full refund.

To Hyeeun—my wife and best friend,
thank you for all that you do.
To my kids—Kennedy, Connery, Cambria,
Kienna and Kolden.
Your are all the absolute best "investments"
I have ever made
I love you all!

TABLE OF CONTENTS

CHAPTER 1

ARE YOU AN "IDIOT" INVESTOR—AND DOES IT MATTER?

"It's a dog eat dog world and I'm wearing Milk Bone underwear."

Norm Peterson (character on Cheers)

My dad dropped out of school at quite a young age and eventually learned how to fix appliances. He was hard-working and eventually opened a used appliance store. During the early 1970s he purchased an acre of rural land on the outskirts of Ottawa and started a hobby farm. Over time the area around our family developed and eventually the homeowners of the newly built houses complained that my dad did not keep his grass cut short enough and that he should remove some trees from his property—so the city bylaw officers were called.

In truth, my dad could be a hard guy to get along with but he was determined he was in the right because he had been living there longer than the new homeowners so he ignored the threats from the city bylaw officers. I was a teenager at this time and one morning as I left for school, I was surprised to see numerous city workers on our property cutting grass and clearing trees. Shortly thereafter, my dad received a bill from the city for the work they had done.

Determined still that he was right, he bought a law book and scoured legal procedures night after night and filed a claim against the city. He argued that not only was he not going to pay for work he did not want done, but he was also suing the city for damage that had occurred to a fence on his property. Everyone laughed at this stubborn fool who had only completed grade 8 arguing against a team of lawyers employed by the city.

But through pit bull determination he won his claim. The city paid him a few thousand dollars for the damage they had done and he was featured in the local newspaper.

I didn't really care about the whole episode at that time, but I learned one important thing—those who care the most often end up winning! In the legal arena, I'm sure my grade 8 educated dad was a complete "idiot" next to these professional lawyers—but the results would seem to indicate otherwise. The lawyers got paid whether they won or not—so what did they care? My dad CARED! I remember that lesson.

Often "idiots" will beat the professionals—
if they care more!

When it comes to creating your wealth, the ultimate responsibility is YOURS. The guy selling you investments might care to a point, but in reality the person who cares the most is the person you see every morning staring back at you when you're looking in the mirror.

This fact is daunting to some people. What do you know about investing? Is it possible that you know more than the people in the financial industry?

Probably not!

However, I'm an "idiot" investor who makes mistakes— but I still managed to amass a net worth of over $1 million in my 30s. This was after spending a good portion of my 20s backpacking across Australia, New Zealand, and Europe and also living in Vancouver and Asia and then leaving the workforce at the age of 34.

The key was that I invested for myself... because I CARED more about MY money than anyone else in the world—and it's the same for you!

The reality is that those in the financial industry get

paid whether or not you make money. The reality of life is that everyone works to benefit themselves first—this fact might be troubling, it might bother you, but it's the truth! You may love your job and be great at it—but the simple truth is that if they stopped paying you, you would stop showing up. It's the same with anyone working in any industry including the financial industry.

So how am I different? I'm not. I sort of stumbled onto writing books after I retired—and it's been fun. I enjoy doing it because I can live my life exactly how I want without all the hassles of working a regular job...BUT ultimately I write books because when people buy them I make a few bucks. It's the same for other writers.

BUT there is one small difference... I am free to give you my unbiased thoughts because I am not paid by any financial company. I am not beholden to the financial industry in any way. I don't receive advertising dollars from various financial firms—which might influence what I choose and don't choose to write about.

So how is this book different from my other books? Let's look at that...

Slight Change in Strategy...

I was able to retire very early by investing in dividend-paying investments and then living off the dividend income. This strategy allows you to collect income regardless of the ups and downs of the stock market. My point was that YOU too could reach financial freedom by focusing on dividends rather than treating stocks like games at a casino—hoping prices would rise.

BUT then something threw a wrench into my best-laid plans...

My book became a National Bestseller. I then wrote a few more bestselling books. The reality is that I was no longer retired and I was earning an income from writing books. Then I stumbled into something else. I began doing paid public speaking engagements which also added to my income. This situation meant that I needed to change my strategy (a little).

Why?

I owned a lot of *high dividend-paying stocks* that were likely to *grow slowly* over the long-term (remember dividends are the cash profitable companies pay share-holders every year). This is a good strategy for retirees who want to live off the dividends received, but it's a poor strategy for people who earn other sources of income—especially for younger people in their 30s.

Why?

Because even though dividend income is taxed favourably, you still have to pay tax on this income every year.

But do you really care about all that? Probably not. How can this information help YOU?

If you are an older investor who is living off the dividends from your portfolio, the original *STOP WORKING* strategy makes the most sense for you. But if you have a job and earn an income and your goal is to build up a dividend income for the future, then you should change things a bit. The reality is:

If you are still working and earning an income, you will be much better off investing in companies that pay a smaller dividend now, but will probably pay much larger dividends in the future.

Let's use an example to show this.

Suppose you wanted to invest some money 10 years ago to create a dependable income stream starting in 2010. You looked at two companies in different industries and you saw that they both had a share price of around $22. One is TransAlta (a utility—and you know that utilities usually have dependable dividends), and the other is Scotiabank. You see that the dividend in 2000 was $1.00 for TransAlta (for almost a 5% yield) versus only $ 0.52 for Scotiabank (about half the dividend rate). It might seem like an easy decision—take the one with the higher dividend! BUT, Scotiabank keeps a portion of their income to grow their business. Look at the years of dividend payments:

Year	TransAlta	Scotiabank
2000	$ 1.00	$ 0.52
2001	$ 1.00	$ 0.66
2002	$ 1.00	$ 0.74
2003	$ 1.00	$ 0.84
2004	$ 1.00	$ 1.02
2005	$ 1.00	$ 1.36
2006	$ 1.00	$ 1.56
2007	$ 1.00	$ 1.79
2008	$ 1.08	$ 1.94
2009	$ 1.16	$ 1.96

Even though TransAlta started with the higher dividend, by growing their business and their earnings, Scotiabank was able to keep growing their dividend over time. In the end Scotiabank's dividend payment is much larger than TransAlta's. So the fact that the dividend grows over time is a huge factor for you! If you had invested 10 years ago for dividend income today, Scotiabank would have been the much better choice.

But a funny thing happens when you focus on buying dependable dividend-payers—you become wealthier! The share price of Scotiabank has more than doubled while TransAlta's share price is pretty much where it was 10 years ago—so your wealth is growing while your dividend income is growing. The point is that you might be able to earn better overall returns *if you don't NEED the dividend income to live on right now.* So let's look at what kinds of stocks make dependable dividend-payers.

CHAPTER 2

EXCELLENT TELEMARKETERS VERSUS MEDIOCRE DOCTORS

"I'm a philosophy major. That means I can think deep thoughts about being unemployed."

—Bruce Lee

Suppose you are considering a career choice (or your child is, if that's closer to the stage of life you're at). You have been accepted to medical school, but during your undergraduate studies you worked as a telemarketer to make extra money. As a telemarketer, you were the best employee the company you worked for had ever seen. You had worked very hard and had managed to meet ever more challenging sales goals. You had become the "Wayne Gretzky" of the telemarketing world! As a doctor, you realize you will be only mediocre—for whatever reason. You will simply do your job in an acceptable manner. Perhaps you are not great at face-to-face communication or maybe your knowledge in sciences is a little shaky. Whatever the reason, you realize that you can either be "the Wayne Gretzky" of telemarketing or a mediocre doctor. Which career choice do you suspect would be the most rewarding from a financial standpoint?

I think the answer is fairly obvious. Telemarketing jobs for the most part are the equivalent of the modern-day sweatshop. I worked as a telemarketer for a short time and it was definitely the worst job I ever had! The pay was very low and I dreaded going to work. The simple truth is that even mediocre doctors will earn a lot more money than even the best telemarketers.

Following along with this simple analogy, certain types of stocks will also earn phenomenally more money for investors than other kinds of stocks—regardless of how good a job their managers do. At least 95% of stocks *are not worth owning at any price*. These are the companies that are similar to the lowly telemarketers—no matter how hard they work or how well they run their business, they earn lousy profits! Even with great management and motivated workers, these companies never earn high returns for their shareholders. As one of the best investors of all-time, Warren Buffett said:

"When a management with a reputation for brilliance tackles a business with a reputation for bad economics, it is usually the reputation of the business that remains intact."

In the hypothetical example of the career choice of being a telemarketer or doctor, those who choose the path of becoming a doctor end up with the financial means to provide their families with fairly comfortable lives. Those who would choose the telemarketing career option end up working hard and struggling but barely making ends meet for their entire working lives. This fact also holds true for stocks—investors who choose wisely finish miles ahead of those who don't. The reality is that by investing in the *best stocks*, you can finish way ahead of investors who choose the rest of the stocks to invest in. This simple choice can make the difference between you ending up very financially secure—or simply scraping by.

Let's take a quick look at the power of investing in the best stocks rather than the rest of the stocks using real-life statistics. Since I have zero interest in spending thousands of hours of my life compiling stock market statistics, let's use statistics that are already available and take a quick look at the data gathered by Jeremy Siegel.

Jeremy Siegel is a professor at the Wharton School of Business and has written a number of books on investing.

In his book, *The Future for Investors*, he shows a lot of empirical evidence about which stocks performed best from 1957-2003. He studied US stocks to create his findings, but similar factors would be true for Canadian stocks as well. From this well-researched data, the best-performing 20 stocks from this timeframe managed to earn an average of over 15% per year compared with the general guideline of 10% per year for the general stock market. So let's assume you invest $100,000 for 25 years at the two different rates of return. What's the approximate difference?

$100,000 invested at 10% for 25 years = $ 1,083,000

$100,000 invested at 15% for 25 years = $ 3,292,000

* The difference between investing in the best and investing in the rest is over $2 million dollars—or over 3 times a much wealth!

That seems easy enough. Simply buy the best investments and end up with millions more in wealth! However, when someone promises to show you how to earn an extra couple million dollars you should be skeptical. The example I gave above has the advantage of 20/20 hindsight. The glaring weakness of the above numbers is that I compared the best stocks to the average stock market *after the results had already been recorded!* The real world does not allow you to go back in time. As much as I enjoyed the movie, *"Back to the Future"*, time travel has not been invented. In a similar vein, I have never bought a lottery ticket in my life, but I would agree to do so if I could choose the numbers on my ticket *after* the numbers had been drawn!

But wait a second... Lottery numbers are drawn pretty much at random from a machine that scrambles the balls—which results in different numbers being chosen each time. But what if there were some *common characteristics* present in the best-performing stocks? If there is a common thread, this would give us an indication of which stocks might perform best in the future.

This sort of approach is similar to looking at the top-paying careers people have and trying to find a common thread. For example, on average dentists, doctors, and lawyers are often much better paid than retail clerks and gas station attendants. I would argue that one of the common threads of the high-paid professions is that they each require extensive training and expertise. So if I was looking to find a highly paid occupation, I might look for those careers which require extensive training because those types of careers usually pay more—that is the common factor that makes these careers a better choice in financial terms.

It's the same with stocks. So let's look a little more closely at Jeremy Siegel's work and see if we can find some common success factors.

CHAPTER 3

LIFE IS NOT FAIR—PROFIT FROM THE CRAPPY TRUTH!

"The most efficient labour-saving device is still money."

—Franklin Jones

It took me a while to realize that the people who work the hardest often end up with the smallest rewards and vice versa. I learned this lesson through my dad's business. My dad quit school after grade 8 because he was not academically inclined, but in many respects—especially in business-related endeavours, he was pretty sharp. As I mentioned earlier, he started a used appliance business which in time grew to be pretty successful. I remember him saying, "These are the people who actually do the work in society—someone has to." In hindsight, after seeing people struggling to hoist appliances up numerous flights of stairs for relatively small pay, I came to the conclusion that indeed, life is not fair.

Going back to our example from the previous chapter, realize that even mediocre doctors almost always earn more than even the best telemarketers. Also realize that this is not *only* because of years of education. I have known a number of people who had PhDs in English or Medieval History who worked minimum wage retail jobs—and they didn't earn any more than high school drop-outs working the same jobs. Education by itself is not the answer.

Doctors have specialized skills that allows them to earn more for their services. In addition, doctors have to be licensed to practice medicine. These two factors limit competition and ensure higher income levels. It's the same with lawyers—they have to be licensed to practice law— and lawyers are generally pretty well-paid. Licensing requirements also apply to many other professions—and these professions offer good financial rewards.

Does government licensing or limiting competition apply to stock investing? Yes. Many companies that have special patents (which prevent other companies from selling the same product for a period of time) often earn very high profits. Pharmaceuticals have benefited for years by patenting their drugs and charging high prices to consumers. This is not a bad thing because these patents encourage companies to develop new medications—with the hope of even greater profits over time.

Many professionals earn higher incomes because they have worked for and have earned the right to add a few extra letters after their names—such as CA (chartered accountant), CMA (Certified Management Accountant, or CGA (Certified General Accountant) in accounting, to CFP for financial planners. There are really countless examples of this, but by adding these letters on your business card, potential clients accept paying up for your services because those letters give them assurances about the quality of your services.

Isn't it the same thing with branded companies? People are often willing to pay a little more for branded products because the brand might assure the customer of a certain level of quality. This brand often allows these companies to charge more for their products (and earn higher profits for investors)! Do you pay more for a Coke or Pepsi than for a store branded soft drink? Of course you do (or at least many people do). BUT, the costs of making a bottle of Coke or Pepsi are not really more than the cost to make store-branded soft drinks—so that is extra profits for these companies. If you can earn an extra dime or quarter on each drink you sell and you are selling billions of drinks—it begins to amount to a lot of money.

With this background information, let's take a quick look at the top performing US stocks from 1957-2003 as shown in Jeremy Siegel's book, *The Future for Investors* along with the returns their investors realized over this timeframe. I've labelled the companies that benefited from either great brands or patents just to show you the power of these factors. At the bottom you can see the average return of the S&P 500 (500 largest stocks in US) during this time.

Company	Annual Return	Competitive Advantages
Philip Morris	19.75%	Strong Brands
Abbott Laboratories	16.51%	Strong Brands/Patents
Bristol Meyers Squibb	16.36%	Strong Brands/Patents
Tootsie Roll Industries	16.11%	Strong Brands
Pfizer	16.03%	Strong Brands/Patents
Coca-Cola	16.02%	Strong Brands
Merck	15.90%	Strong Brands/Patents
PepsiCo	15.54%	Strong Brands
Colgate-Palmolive	15.22%	Strong Brands
Crane	15.14%	
H.J. Heinz	14.78%	Strong Brands
Wrigley	14.65%	Strong Brands
Fortune Brands	14.55%	Strong Brands
Kroger	14.41%	

Schering-Plough	14.36%	Strong Brands/Patents
Procter & Gamble	14.26%	Strong Brands
Hershey	14.22%	Strong Brands
Wyeth	13.99%	Strong Brands/Patents
Royal Dutch Shell	13.64%	
General Mills	13.58%	Strong Brands

Average return per year of these stocks: 15.26%

Average return for S&P stocks per year: 10.85%

* Note: The S&P is simply a list of the largest companies in the US.

Remember from the previous chapter, the difference in results for investors who saved $100,000 and blindly invested in the general stock market for 25 years versus the investors who saved the same $100,000 but instead invested in these top-20 companies was huge! This minor change in approach created a gain of over *$2 million for investors who chose the best stocks!* By reviewing the data and looking at what special competitive advantages these companies had, there were a couple of common threads with these outperforming stocks:

1. The vast majority of the top-performing stocks had strong brands
2. Most of the remaining top-performing stocks had patent protection.

Many people assume it is too difficult to find long-term winning stocks—but I disagree! Indeed it does take a little more work at the beginning to find these great companies, but once the initial legwork is done, the best approach is to simply allow these great companies to keep operating their businesses while increasing their profits—and paying you more dividends! It's similar to our doctor/telemarketer example. Medical school is very tough, but once you are completed, you are virtually guaranteed a fairly comfortable income for the rest of your working life while the telemarketer will have to jump through hoops and keep performance numbers up forever simply to eke out a meagre existence.

Of course many people will immediately parrot the words seen on most financial literature that, *"Past returns are no guarantee of future results"*, but if there is a common factor that allows companies to outperform over time, isn't it worth a look? I mean if you like a certain restaurant and you always go there because you like it, aren't you relying on past experiences to make your decision? Let's approach investing the same way and see if we can perhaps find some of the "best stocks". In keeping with this idea, the next chapter will look a little more closely at exactly what makes a great quality stock—a stock that will continue to increase earnings and dividends in good times and bad. A stock that will prosper regardless of who is running the company. In short—"idiot-proof" stocks...

CHAPTER 4

ONLY INVEST IN "IDIOT-PROOF" STOCKS

" Success is more a function of consistent common sense than it is of genius."

—An Wang

One of the key messages that Warren Buffett has delivered numerous times is that investors are well served by buying stocks in great quality companies—and then simply holding on and benefiting from their investments. I would love to tell you that I have mastered the art of timing my investments based on some set of economic data, but that would be totally untrue. *I have no clue* what the stock markets are going to do over the next year (or five years), but over time good quality companies will reward investors. I am the *worst* market-timer in the world, but fortunately this shortcoming has not had a huge impact on my returns over time.

Don't Take My Word for It—What Do I Know?

I love stocks as they helped me escape the rat race at 34 and become financially comfortable—but maybe I was simply lucky. How can you be fairly confident that stocks will work well for you too over the long-term?

First off, nothing in life is certain. You could make all the plans in the world and they could be irrevocably altered in a blink of an eye. However, as with most things, you should probably play the odds. Getting more education does not *guarantee* you better employment prospects, but the odds favour this so that is why many people go on to post-secondary studies of some sort even though the costs in both time and money are huge. Many statistics support the argument that in most cases the time and money invested in extra education is worth it— both financially and in other ways.

When it comes to stocks—you want to be "shown the money". If we look at stocks, history has shown that stocks are a great long-term investment. If you like to read telephone directory sized books filled with incredible amounts of empirical data on investing, I would highly recommend you get a copy of Jeremy Siegel's book, *Stocks for the Long Run* which supports the idea of investing in stocks. If reading intense financial books is not your idea of fun, I will summarize the basic idea of the book:

> *Over the long-term, stocks have returned much more to investors than investments such as bonds, banks accounts, treasury bonds, and gold.*

If you would like more information about how stocks have performed over time, I would suggest you read, *Dividends Still Don't Lie* by Kelley Wright where he shows that from 1926–2008, the US stock market has performed better than bonds in 62 of 64 20-year periods, or 96.8% of the time. During the same period, stocks outperformed bonds about 86% of the time during 10 year periods. In this case, the numbers don't lie.

Think about it. The reason car insurance companies charge higher rates to young drivers is because *the odds are that young drivers are more likely to have an accident.* They can't predict the future any better than the rest of us, but history has shown this to be the case, so that's how they have managed to earn decent profits—by betting with the odds!

I would argue that the world with regards to investing has not changed that much over time and the next number of decades will look similar to the last number of decades. Although future returns might be lower than some investors have come to expect, overall people are still putting one pant leg on before the other and working and supporting their families. The problems we have today seem so big because we are living them right now, but I'm sure they are not any larger than when our parents or grandparents worried about the Nazis conquering the world or what the USSR was going to do during the Cold War. Life is never perfect and there are always problems—but somehow we muddle through and do okay. Over time standards of living have risen and life has gotten better for large parts of humanity and I still think this trend will continue. I am optimistic *long-term* and if that optimism is well-placed, stocks will be the place to invest.

What Stocks Should You Buy Then?

If stocks are the best passive investment option (and I would argue they are as history shows), then what kind of stocks should you buy?

Only invest in *Quality* Stocks. But what is a quality stock? From my experience, great quality stocks are usually found with companies that have survived and even thrived for many decades. These companies crank out good profits every year and in many cases they reward their shareholders by paying out ever-increasing dividends (the regular cash shareholders receive). Over 95% of stocks are garbage—so how can you find the great 5% of stocks to invest in?

Let's start with the nine criteria I listed in my first book:

1. Companies that you can easily understand.
2. Companies that pay a dividend (preferably a rising one).
3. Stocks that are selling cheaply (the old adage of "buy low")
4. Companies that are recession-proof
5. Focus on North American companies (because you are familiar with them)
6. Companies that are dominant in their industries.
7. Companies with a long history of great performance.
8. Companies that command strong brand loyalty.
9. Once you've bought the perfect company, don't sell it!

This was the basic criteria I followed to invest and leave the rat race at the age of 34. I already explained all these concepts in my first book, so I won't repeat them here. I still believe in these criteria, but over time I

continue to learn and grow—as we all do. So, I would add
a few other criteria. Invest in companies that:

10. Offer products or services that are purchased
    often, rather than only once.
11. Will be able to keep recording good profits even
    as things change.
12. Companies that regularly buy back their own
    shares.
13. Are very PROFITABLE—the ONLY reason
    companies exist.

I would also add a word of caution about:

1. Financial companies—many have done very well
   for shareholders over long periods of time, but
   they do take on more risk than many other types
   of businesses.
2. Companies that rely on patents for their profits
   as patents do expire after a certain time period.

Let's take a quick look at the new criteria I am adding as
I have never written about these before:

Offer products or services that are purchased often:
All else being equal, I would rather buy a company that

sells you a product or service you use regularly rather than a company that sells you something you need once in a long while. From the list of the best-performing stocks since 1957, notice that the absolute best performing stock was Philip Morris (the maker of cigarettes). Is there any other product in existence that people consume with the same regularity as cigarettes? I would argue that this is one of the main reasons tobacco companies have been such good investments over time—you buy cigarettes and use them up quickly and then go out and buy some more... every day!

As a quick comparison to see how powerful this fact is, look at the difference between investing in the US market as a whole and investing in Philip Morris stock from 1957-2003. During this time the "market" managed to earn 10.75% per year, while Philip Morris earned 19.75% annually. Take a quick look at the difference (we'll use an initial investment of only $1,000 to keep the final numbers smaller:

Investing in "the US market" @ 10.85% per year = $113,000

Investing in Philip Morris @ 19.75% per year = $3,987,000

The difference in huge—over 30 times as much wealth! The whole idea of investing in companies that garner repeat sales being a great investment idea is not the *only* reason Philip Morris did so well, but let's take a quick minute to review the 20 best-performing stocks in the US market from 1957-2003. The list is full of companies that get repeat sales of their products. In fact the list is filled with soft drink companies, drug companies, and food companies—all things you use regularly. In total, 19 of the 20 best performing stocks were of companies that sell products people buy regularly.

So how can you use this information? Well, if you are a cell phone junkie, don't invest in the manufacturer of your cell phone (a one-time purchase), but invest instead in the company that provides your cell phone service—don't you use their service every day and send them a payment every month? If you drive, NEVER invest in the company that manufactured your car (history is littered with bankrupt automobile manufacturers) but instead invest in the oil companies that provide the fuel to run your car—which you buy regularly. The truth is that companies that sell products or services people robotically buy generally make great long-term investments. This simple investing idea is worth remembering.

Companies that will earn profits
even as things change

Invest in companies whose products don't really change over time. It's been said that the only constant in life is

change—and this is true. The last 100 years has seen countless transformations to our way of life. For example, a
computer that was as large as an entire building 40 years
ago would have the same computing power as a device that
would sit on your desk today. The reality is that technology
advances over time and these changes affect our lives—but
can also affect our investments.

For example, Kodak was (and still is) synonymous
with photography. For years Eastman Kodak churned out
good profits by developing film—then something
happened...the invention of the digital camera. Investors
who paid $80 per share or more in the 1990s for shares in
Kodak hoping to collect the dividends were sorely
disappointed as Kodak has now eliminated its dividend.
To add insult to injury, if they now decided to sell those
shares, they would only receive $3-$4 as of this writing.
This simple fact is important:

> *Technology is fast-changing and hard to predict—so
> DON'T invest in technology companies unless you
> have some personal insight in that area.*

Remember, I'm an "idiot" millionaire. I have no clue
what the future holds, so I stick to things that don't
change over time. I would rather invest in potato chips
than computer chips. The reality is that regardless of how

technology changes, people will still consume simple products.

But it's not just technology that can cause investors trouble. Years ago consumer branded companies that filled the aisles of supermarkets were virtual cash machines. Then retailers got smart and started offering store brands (at much cheaper prices). As this happened, many of the branded companies' profits became much harder to come by. This is why with food companies I *generally* prefer to buy companies that offer impulse products that are relatively inexpensive. The reality is that consumers' mindsets change as soon as they enter a supermarket—they become very price-conscious. This simple reality means that it becomes more difficult for companies to extract higher profits for their products because if they price their offerings too high, people choose the store brands. Contrast that to the rows of chocolate bars you see at the local convenience store. They are not always cheap, but the consumer sees it and buys it on impulse—ensuring large profit margins for the manufacturer. This is one of the main reasons that Kraft (which has a huge cheese business) bought Cadbury (which owns many chocolate bar brands). Think about it—when was the last time you purchased a store brand chocolate bar? Probably never. Store branded cheese? I buy it often. So chocolate bars offer more profit than cheese.

This does not mean that companies that compete solely based on price are always bad investments. Companies that compete on price can be great investments *if they are the lowest cost producer.* Wal-Mart is one of the world's most valuable companies and it has made its fortune by squeezing inefficiencies out of the retailing landscape.

The main point is to look for companies that operate in such a way that technology or other changes will not affect their profitability.

Companies that regularly buy back their own shares

This is an important factor I look for with investing in the stocks. However, in order to fully understand my thinking on this, you have to understand my investment approach with regards to the stage in the life cycle a company is at. Chapter 20 will explain all this in detail.

PROFITS—the *ONLY* reason companies exist.

As a shareholder, your financial fortunes are tied to how much profit the companies you invest in are able to earn. You want companies that can earn healthy profits over time—and pay you rising dividends. But the fact of the matter is that many companies can't earn healthy profits and are continually running on the proverbial treadmill just to stay in business. The reality is that:

Companies with the largest profits have the happiest shareholders.

So how can companies earn large profits—and make you happy? The easiest way is if they can earn a higher profit from each sale rather than trying in increase sales. Let's use a fictional example to explain. Suppose Company A and Company B produce similar products that cost 95 cents to make and they sell for $1 (in other words their profit on each item sold is 5 cents. Each company sells 1 million items a year.

Profits:

Company A: ($0.05 profit) x 1,000,000 units sold = $ 50,000

Company B: ($0.05 profit) x 1,000,000 units sold = $ 50.000

Their profits are identical. Then the CEOs of both companies decide that they want to make their shareholders happier, so they each devise a plan to increase profits. The CEO of Company A creates a plan to increase sales by 100% through various promotions. The CEO of Company B creates a plan that makes customers value his product and as a result is able to charge 25% more for his product (but the amount he sells stays the same). Look at the results if:

Company A increases sales by 100% (to 2,000,000 units)

Company B increases prices by only 25%

   (so profit climbs to 30 cents/unit)

Profits:

Company A: ($0.05 profit) x 2,000,000 units sold = $100,000

Company B: ($0.30 profits) x 1,000,000 units sold = $ 300,000

* The profits from Company A have doubled while the profits from Company B have gone up six-fold!

In the real world it is very hard to devise a plan where you can suddenly raise your prices, BUT companies that can sell products with higher profits per unit make MUCH more money over time.

Let's move on and give you a real-life example using actual companies—one crummy business versus a great one. The crummy business (Alcoa) is the largest aluminum producer in the US and it sells a commodity product, so it competes based on price. The second company sells a branded product (Coca Cola) in which it can charge higher prices to customers. Think about it...a lot of that Coke people drink come in aluminum cans. The buyers of aluminum want the best price—period! But the buyers of colas will pay more for certain brands. Next time you're at a Wal-Mart, take a look at the vending machines in front of the store. You can buy a Wal-Mart branded soft drink for 35 cents whereas the Coke (or Pepsi) will cost you $1.50 or more. The costs to produce these products is similar...the difference in price is because of the power of the brand. That extra money people pay goes straight to the profit of Coke or Pepsi shareholders. So let's look at the 10-year per share financials of Alcoa versus Coca Cola:

Year	Alcoa Earnings	Alcoa Dividend	Coca Cola Earnings	Coca Cola Dividend
2000	$ 1.81	$ 0.50	$ 1.48	$ 0.68
2001	$ 1.46	$ 0.60	$ 1.60	$ 0.72
2002	$ 0.92	$ 0.60	$ 1.65	$ 0.80
2003	$ 1.21	$ 0.60	$ 1.95	$ 0.88
2004	$ 1.53	$ 0.60	$ 2.06	$ 1.00
2005	$ 1.43	$ 0.60	$ 2.17	$ 1.12
2006	$ 2.90	$ 0.60	$ 2.37	$ 1.24
2007	$ 2.95	$ 0.68	$ 2.57	$ 1.36
2008	$ 0.28	$ 0.68	$ 3.02	$ 1.52
2009	(–$ 1.06)	$ 0.26	$ 2.93	$ 1.64

Both of these companies have been in business for over a century, but while Alcoa's profits and dividends are erratic, Coke's profits and dividends tend to gradually increase over time. Realize too that this was during a time when commodity prices were soaring (which should help

Alcoa and hurt Coca Cola). Which company's stock would you rather own?

Companies can generate high profits in a few different ways such as:

- charging customers more for their products (strong brands)
- being super-efficient and thus having low costs (think Wal-Mart)
- charging high prices because the company has a product that competitors can't replicate (a monopoly or oligopoly)

The important fact to remember is that profits (not sales) are the name of the game with investing.

Now on to a few big lessons I learned during the turmoil in 2008. Invest cautiously with:

Financial companies:

Banking and insurance can be great businesses—but I have learned to be a little more cautious. If we start by looking at banking, this can be a great business where the company does not have to produce or store any products. The basic model is that banks borrow cheaply and lend at expensive rates. Their profits are based on the difference.

The trouble with banks is that they carry tremendous amounts of debt on their balance sheets—which can really blow up in the event of an economic downturn (like we experienced in 2008–2009). One idiotic move I made was by investing in Bank of America. This former dividend all-star made some stupid acquisitions at the height of the financial panic and ran into tremendous difficulty. As a result the stock plummeted and the dividend was cut massively. Here in Canada, our banks have some advantages US banks don't have. For example, rather than having thousands of smaller banks as in the US, we have a handful of very large chartered banks along with some smaller players. This fact makes the market more profitable for the established banks as consumers have fewer options when price shopping. In addition, the rules which relate to mortgage defaults are more favourable for our Canadian banks. Regardless, the fact that banks carry a tremendous amount of debt on their balance sheets have made me become a little more cautious in this area.

As banks were being propped up in the US during the financial crisis, AIG (the world's largest insurance company) was also on the verge of bankruptcy. This company ran into tremendous difficulty and these problems also crept into Canada with Manulife—Canada's largest insurance company. This company offered complicated guarantees to many investors based on the stock market performance and these guarantees cost them dearly as the stock market crashed. The result was their stock price plummeted and their dividend was cut in half.

All this does not mean I will never invest in financial companies as these companies have been virtual cash machines for many years, but lessons learned from the financial crisis will make me more cautious in the future.

Companies that rely on patents:

If you were looking for a great performing industry over the last number of decades, the pharmaceutical industry would stand out as a top performer. These companies spend billions of dollars to develop drugs to treat illnesses. When they create a successful drug, they patent it and receive the exclusive right to sell the medicine for many years. The potential trouble with this business model is that after a period of time, these patents expire and generic companies move in and offer similar products at much cheaper prices. So in essence patents are very valuable when they are received, but their value gradually declines over time. If too many patents expire without a company replacing them with new discoveries that can be patented, once stalwart dividend-paying companies become weakened and may be forced to cut their dividends.

So with the original 9 investing tenets mentioned in

my first book combined with these new criteria, let's look at the best quality stocks you might consider investing in. I call these the list of "idiot-proof" stocks, because if you buy them cheaply, you can probably just tuck them away and watch the dividends roll in (and rise over time) while you slowly become wealthy. Here's the list...

THE IDIOT MILLIONAIRE'S LIST OF... "IDIOT-PROOF" STOCKS

CHAPTER 5

NOTHING LIKE LOONIES IN THE BANK!

"I hate banks. They do nothing positive fore anybody except themselves. They're first in with their fees and first out when there's trouble."
—**Harvey Goldsmith**

Even though I am a little more cautious about financial companies because they take on a lot of debt in their regular course of business, I still like Canadian chartered banks. The simple truth is that many banks make money and Canadian chartered banks make a *lot* of money! The term "chartered bank refers to the fact that banks receive their charter from the federal government under the Bank Act. In Canada the market is dominated by the "big five" banks—which creates an oligopoly. An oligopoly means that there are a few dominant players who can exert control over the market.

As a customer, you realize the various ways the banks are able to separate you from your money. You gripe and complain but still you bank with them—because you have no choice! Every year you get a notice telling you which service fees are being increased and you pay them. Everybody else also pays these fees and all those dollars quickly add up to billions! In addition, when you consider that a mortgage is the biggest expense most people face (aside from taxes) and you realize that the majority of people have a mortgage on their house at some point in their lives, you truly begin to appreciate the earning potential of the big banks You can't go too far wrong investing in Canadian banks.

Their Advantage

Banking is really just a commodity business. By this I mean if one bank offers a better price or service, people will choose to go there. Regardless of which bank you do business with, the colour of the money they dispense is all the same. However, the advantage banks have is that it is a real pain to try to switch banks. Once you have your mortgage, credit cards and direct deposits going to your bank—there are a host of problems that can arise if you switch. What if there is a problem with your paycheque and it goes astray? What if your billing information gets lost? It's not impossible to change banks and save money—but it's a lot more difficult than simply going to a different store to buy a product that's on sale. The benefits of switching can be unknown because another bank might save you money in one area, but charge you more somewhere else to make up the difference. Newer online banks offer very attractive prices on some services, but there is the inconvenience of not having an actual branch to deal with if you need to do something a little more complex than simple deposits and withdrawals.

Potential Risks
During the 2008-2009 financial crisis, our Canadian banks became shining examples of well-managed, conservative banks. However, you must realize that banks are in the business of borrowing and lending money and they lend out way more than they keep on deposit. As such, they are susceptible to bad management and taking on too much risk. Our banks have made some horrible mistakes in the past and that is the main risk you take with investing in financial companies. Fortunately (for bank shareholders), whenever banks have made financial mistakes, they have been able to make up the profit shortfall by raising service fees. The reality in Canada is that there are really only a handful of massive banks and

they all charge similar prices for their products. As such, the words "record profits" are the sweet music Canadian bank investors have become accustomed to hearing. Overall, Canadian banks are a reasonable area to invest in, but don't over-commit. By this I mean you should not invest your entire portfolio in bank shares. Believe it or not, I have met a few people who have mentioned that they *only* invest in banks.

A few that I like:

1. RBC Financial (symbol RY—Canada)

Started in 1864 as The Merchants Bank by a group of Halifax Merchants, Royal bank steadily grew and today is the largest Canadian bank with strong businesses in Canadian and International banking as well as Wealth Management, Capital Markets, and Insurance. It currently has over 18 million personal, business, and institutional clients. Numerous recent acquisitions have extended the company's presence into the US market and the bank continues to expand its army of financial advisors. This company has rewarded shareholders tremendously well over many decades and this should continue in the future. Here's a quick look at the dividend history over the last 10 years:

Year	Dividend/Share
2000	$ 0.57
2001	$ 0.69
2002	$ 0.76
2003	$ 0.86
2004	$ 1.01
2005	$ 1.17
2006	$ 1.48
2007	$ 1.82
2008	$ 2.00
2009	$ 2.00

You will notice that during the last year, RBC did not raise its dividend. However, this is probably only temporary as the economy works its way through the current financial problems. This has been a great stock to own over time and the factors that have made it a great stock are still in place.

2. TD Canada Trust (symbol TD—Canada)

TD got its start as The Bank of Toronto in 1855. Today it is the second largest bank in Canada and the sixth largest in North America after completing the $8 billion acquisition of Canada Trust. Recently it has been expanding in the US market in addition to adding to its other lines of business. A dominating player in the discount brokerage market in

Canada, TD has rewarded shareholders very well over time. Here's the 10-year dividend history:

Year	Dividend/Share
2000	$ 0.92
2001	$ 1.09
2002	$ 1.12
2003	$ 1.16
2004	$ 1.36
2005	$ 1.58
2006	$ 1.78
2007	$ 2.11
2008	$ 2.36
2009	$ 2.44

3. Scotiabank (symbol BNS—Canada)

Founded in Halifax in 1832 under the name Bank of Nova Scotia, Scotiabank is perhaps Canada's most international bank. This bank opened its first foreign branch over 100 years ago in 1885 and this global expansion continues today as the bank has a strong presence in Mexico, El Salvador, Costa Rica, Chile, Peru and Venezuela as well as many other countries around the world. The bank is very profitable and has managed to reward shareholders over the years with dividend increases in 37 of the last 39 years. Here's how dividends have increased over the last 10 years:

Year	Dividend/Share
2000	$ 0.50
2001	$ 0.62
2002	$ 0.73
2003	$ 0.84
2004	$ 1.10
2005	$ 1.32
2006	$ 1.50
2007	$ 1.74
2008	$ 1.92
2009	$ 1.96

* Note—Scotiabank is one of the companies I highlighted in my book, *The Lazy Investor* about DRIPping (dividend reinvesting). In 2008, the bank sweetened the deal for shareholders who DRIP offering a 2% discount off the share price of all reinvested dividends. This policy may be terminated in the future if the bank no longer feels the need for extra liquidity (cash), but small investors should take advantage while they can.

You really can't go wrong investing in any of Canada's major banks (and even some of the smaller ones), but the three listed above have visible growth strategies and I feel they are the best within this very profitable industry. Once again, the only word of caution would be to be aware that these companies do carry a lot of debt as that is the nature of their business. I have learned through painful experience to avoid US banks as the competition in that market is fierce and the risks are too high for me—so I'll avoid that area of the market.

CHAPTER 6

OTHER FINANCIAL COMPANIES

"There are worse things in life than death.
Have you ever spent an evening with an
insurance salesman?"
—Woody Allen

Within Canada, financial companies have been great places to invest over time. The banks have been wonderful places to grow your wealth, but other financial companies have also been great wealth generators. There are a few major insurance companies such as Manulife, Sun Life, and Great West Life along with various mutual fund companies such as Investor's Group. The financial crisis highlighted some of the risks carried by these types of companies as the largest insurer in the world, AIG, had to be backstopped by the US government.

Their Advantage

Financial companies such as insurance or mutual fund firms have some distinct benefits over other types of companies. For starters, most of them operate with agents who only get paid when they make a sale. In addition, these agents will often meet clients right at their homes to provide personal service. This business model keeps overhead low. Apart from the administration staff, these companies can avoid spending enormous sums of money on huge buildings and fixed salaries. If sales slow down, it's the agents who bear the brunt of the slowdown as they earn fewer commissions.

In addition, once people sign up for an investment plan or insurance plan, they are not likely to switch easily—so the customers tend to stick with these companies and continue to pay their policies or invest in their financial plans year after year—generating fee income for these companies. This fact has allowed these companies to generate healthy profits over many years.

Potential Risks

Companies that offer exotic financial products can end up in a difficult position during bad economic times. AIG (formerly the largest insurance company in the world) bet heavily on credit default swaps (essentially guaranteeing payment on debt) and would have gone bankrupt had they not been bailed out by the US government. Financial companies sometimes do these sorts of things because it seems like an easy road to riches. Be aware that trouble can happen in Canada too. Manulife offered guaranteed products linked to the performance of the stock market and suffered huge losses as a result.

Let's look at one dominant Canadian financial company which is controlled by one of Canada's wealthiest families. Then we'll look at an example of a company that does not bear the regular risk most financial companies face—but still manages to earn great profits!

1. Power Financial (symbol PWF—Canada)

Controlled by one of the wealthiest families in Canada (the Desmarais family), Power Financial has majority ownership of the largest mutual fund company in Canada (Investor's Group) and one of the largest insurers (Great-West Life). This company is conservatively managed but has still managed to generate wealth for investors. Here's a snapshot of the approximate 10-year dividend track record:

Year	Dividend/Share
2000	$ 0.36
2001	$ 0.43
2002	$ 0.52
2003	$ 0.70
2004	$ 0.72
2005	$ 0.87
2006	$ 1.00
2007	$ 1.16
2008	$ 1.33
2009	$ 1.40

Within the US market there are countless financial companies—and I would avoid most of them. This does not mean that they would not make great investments, it's just that after the financial crisis I would want to make sure my money is a secure as possible—and I just don't feel that I have enough assurances to make an investment outside of Canada. In addition, financial companies are one area of the market where Canadians have a pretty good selection of domestic investment opportunities—so why make extra efforts to invest outside our borders?

Some other notable companies that might be worth looking at include Sun Life and Manulife. Manulife has had some recent problems (offering guaranteed products based on the performance of the stocks market) which has really hurt its profits and hammered its stock price, so there may be some value there...but there are also some risks.

2. Visa Inc (symbol V—US)

If you are over the age of 18, chances are you have a credit card. We have credit cards from stores, gas stations and other places, but the most common credit card by far is Visa. The reason I like this card company is that *they do not lend money to their customers.* Visa is merely an electronics payment network. Visa makes money by charging banks to issue its cards and charging merchants for taking the card. That is why you see so many various credit card offers—it's the banks who determine the rate of interest charged to cardholders. If you only make the minimum payment each month, then it's the issuing bank that reaps the high interest income off of you. If you declare bankruptcy and never pay your bill, it's the bank that loses money. All the risks (and potential rewards) are the responsibility of the issuing bank.

Visa earns their money whether you pay your Visa bill or not! It is not the one lending you money with your credit card. This removes some risk (and also potential profit) from Visa.

So as long as people keep using plastic to make their purchases, this company will continue to make money. Since its introduction in 1958, Visa has grown such that there are currently over 1.5 billion Visa cards in circulation in over 170 countries. These cards were used to purchases trillions of dollars in goods and services—and Visa gets a small slice of all these transactions. As world population is expected to increase by another couple of billion residents and as many of these individuals become wealthier, Visa will earn more money.

As an aside, realize that Visa is different than American Express because when you use your Amex card, it is American Express who is lending you the money and taking on the risk. This is why I would prefer to own shares of Visa rather than Amex—the risk is lower. However, MasterCard operates in the same way that Visa does—they only operate a network and don't lend money. BUT I would prefer to own Visa because it is more dominant. Worldwide, it is estimated that Visa's market share of debit and credit card transactions is 68% compared with only 28% for MasterCard. I usually prefer the dominant players and even though the future looks bright for MasterCard, I would prefer investing in the "king of the hill"—and that is Visa.

CHAPTER 7

PIPELINE TO PROFITS

"They're all making love lying up against the pipeline and you got thousands of caribou up there.

—George H.W. Bush,
speaking about the Alaskan pipeline

Pipelines have got to be one of the simpler businesses out there. Essentially, if you have a lot of oil or natural gas in one area and a lot of customers a long way away, the most efficient way to transport the resource is through a pipeline. Pipelines are fairly conservative investments whose earnings are not really affected by the ups and downs of the economy—or oil and gas prices. The simple reality is that if it's minus 30 degrees outside, you *are* going to heat your home! This reality makes these types of companies worth investigating. Realize that over time they will probably grow more slowly than some of the other types of stocks I've listed here, but they still offer pretty good low-risk returns over the long-term.

Their Advantage

Building a pipeline costs millions of dollars and lots of regulatory hurdles must be cleared before construction can take place. These factors make building a pipeline a difficult undertaking. However, the beauty of this enormous cost and effort is that once a pipeline is built, the company has a virtual monopoly until there is enough demand to justify another pipeline being built. Although the rates pipelines can charged are regulated, overall there are steady, safe profits to be had—and nice juicy dividends.

Potential Risks

At the time of this writing, interest rates are hovering around generational lows. Interest rates will have to climb at some point, and this will negatively affect the stock prices of pipeline companies to a degree. This does not mean the dividends will decrease if interest rates rise, but stock prices might fall or remain stagnant.

A few good candidates

1. Enbridge (symbol ENB—Canada)

One of my favourite conservative Canadian stocks, Enbridge, is focused on three core businesses—oil pipelines, natural gas pipelines and natural gas distribution. People NEED this company virtually every day of their lives. As a result, this company has managed to generate good returns for shareholders. As a quick illustration of this, over the last 50 years Enbridge has managed to generate an average return of 12.9% per year versus 9.7% per year for the Canadian stock market in general—a HUGE difference. Once again, if we invested $100,000 into these two different investments (either Enbridge or the general stock market) for 25 years—look at the difference (below):

Stock Market:$100,000 @ 9.7% for 25 years = $ 1,012,000

Enbridge:$100,000 @ 12.9% for 25 years = $ 2,077,000

* By choosing Enbridge, investors would have earned over $1 million extra! These returns would also have been realized with a fairly low-risk stock. The company has paid dividends for 57 years. Let's take a quick look at the 10-year dividend history:

Year	Dividend/Share
2000	$ 0.64
2001	$ 0.70
2002	$ 0.76
2003	$ 0.83
2004	$ 0.92
2005	$ 1.04
2006	$ 1.15
2007	$ 1.23
2008	$ 1.32
2009	$ 1.48

* Note: Enbridge is a company that my children own shares in and they are enrolled in DRIPs (dividend reinvestment). Investors who reinvest dividends receive a 2% discount on the shares they purchase.

2. TransCanada Corp (symbol TRP—Canada)

TransCanada operates a network of over 60,000 kms of pipeline as well as gas storage operations which have the capacity for over 380 billion cubic feet of storage. Once again, this company provides a service that is vital to the functioning of our modern economy and the dividend payments have been pretty consistent (with the exception of the dividend cut in 1999—which has been more than fully restored since). Here's a quick look at the last ten years of dividend payments:

Year	Dividend/Share
2000	$ 0.80
2001	$ 0.90
2002	$ 1.00
2003	$ 1.08
2004	$ 1.16
2005	$ 1.22
2006	$ 1.28
2007	$ 1.36
2008	$ 1.44
2009	$ 1.52

3. Pembina Pipelines (symbol PPL—Canada)

Pembina Pipelines used to be an income trust but converted to a corporation in late 2010. As a corporation, Pembina will have to start paying tax like a regular corporation. This company will probably grow more slowly than Enbridge and Trans-Canada in the future, but it does offer a higher dividend yield right now. Also be aware that the dividend might be cut some time in the future, but overall it should remain fairly generous. It might be prudent to watch this company and invest if you see a dividend cut that might materialize within the next few years. If the stock price is affected by the cut, it could be an opportune time to buy. Here's a quick snapshot of the 10-year dividend history:

Year	Dividend/Share
2000	$ 0.96
2001	$ 1.05
2002	$ 1.05
2003	$ 1.05
2004	$ 1.05
2005	$ 1.05
2006	$ 1.16
2007	$ 1.37
2008	$ 1.49
2009	$ 1.56

Generally speaking, pipeline companies offer a necessary service and operate with virtual monopolies (albeit regulated by the government). There are other pipeline companies that operate in Canada, but these ones are large and established—with pretty good track records.

CHAPTER 8

SMOKIN' PROFITS

Giving up smoking is easy...
I've done it hundreds of times."
—**Mark Twain**

Tobacco traces its origins to the Americas before the Europeans arrived. Today, over 15 billion cigarettes are smoked every day all around the world. While consumption has been gradually falling in many developed countries, consumption is increasing in many developing countries. Some people have an ethical aversion to investing in tobacco stocks, so if you do, please skip over this section. I have five children and I would not want any of them to smoke, but the reality is that some people will decide to smoke whether we have a legal industry or not. Prohibition did not eliminate alcohol consumption and the "war on drugs" has done very little to curb the inclination of some people to choose that vice, so outlawing tobacco seems like a silly, knee-jerk idea. Having said that, I fully support marketing bans and increased taxation to curtail the appeal of smoking (especially for kids). If you are a smoker or do not have an ethical aversion to other people choosing to smoke, tobacco companies have provided investors with phenomenal returns over the decades.

Their Advantage

This is by far the best consumer product ever invented from an investor standpoint. Brand loyalty is extremely high. Think about it—when you see someone ask for a pack of cigarettes, do you notice that they ask for a specific brand? In addition, a pack of cigarettes is very cheap to produce, so the profit margins are enormous! The reality is that even though overall smoking rates have declined in North America from 1-3% per year over the last few decades, price increases have more than made up for reduced demand, so overall company *profits* keep going up! In addition, consumers continue to buy more of the product every day or two—so the companies receive a regular infusion of cash. Finally, this is the one industry where advertising restrictions have actually cemented the positions of the dominant firms as it is now virtually impossible for a new brand to steal market share.

Potential Risks

Lawsuits and further restrictions on tobacco use are a risk faced by the tobacco industry. The reality is that cigarettes are not good for people's health, so there is little sympathy when governments announce increased taxation or further restrictions on where the products can be consumed.

Often when speaking at various events, listeners have questioned my interest in investing in tobacco companies. Won't governments drive them out of business eventually? My reply is always the same. Governments do not really want people to stop smoking because if they did, tax revenues would fall. This is one area where tax increases are generally not opposed by the public, so they are an easy source of revenue for governments.

A few good candidates

1. Philip Morris International
    (symbol PM—US)

Over the last couple of decades, US tobacco companies have been hit with a barrage of lawsuits. This unending litigation created a unique situation where Altria (the maker of Marlboro cigarettes among others) divided itself into two distinct companies—Altria and Philip Morris International. Now Altria has the rights to the top-selling brands (including Marlboro) inside the United States whereas Philip Morris International has the rights to these brands everywhere else on the globe (away from the US—the lawsuit capital of the world). This was the fastest-growing part of the original Philip Morris (renamed Altria) company, so over time, Philip Morris International should be a growth machine. The interesting thing about this split is that Canadian investors can buy the shares in New York using US dollars, but none of the company's earnings come from within the US. In other words, you can buy it cheaply when the US dollar is weak, but the profits are still earned in other foreign countries—so this company offers a unique way for Canadian investors to use their relatively strong currency to invest in foreign profits.

Let's take a quick look at the difference with $100,000 invested for 25 years at the rate Philip Morris has managed to return to shareholders (19.75%) versus the market average of (10.85%):

Stock Market Average: $100,000 @ 10.85% for 25 years = $ 1,313,000

Philip Morris: $100,000 @ 19.75% for 25 years = $ 9,055,000

* Over 25 years, an investor earning the average returns from 1957-2003 would have earned almost **$8 million** extra by investing in Philip Morris instead of the overall stock market!

Since this company was only spun off in 2008, it does not have a long dividend history—but the old Philip Morris was a great dividend machine, so this new international version should reward shareholders as well. Since 2008, the company has raised its dividend twice by a total of 26%! For interest, let's take a look at the dividend history for the last 10 years before the spin off:

Year	Dividend/Share
1997	$ 1.60
1998	$ 1.68
1999	$ 1.84
2000	$ 2.02
2001	$ 2.22
2002	$ 2.44
2003	$ 2.64
2004	$ 2.82
2005	$ 3.06
2006	$ 3.32

The reality is that this company is the 800-pound gorilla in the international tobacco market and it should continue to gain market share for many years. There are more Marlboro cigarettes consumed every year internationally than the next three brands combined. In addition, although the percentage of smokers is declining in many areas of the world, the world population is projected to grow to almost 9 billion people by 2050, so there will be more smokers overall. I gained respect for this company when I noticed that every time I was on an international flight, the most common product travellers stocked up on was Marlboro cigarettes. This company has done extremely well for investors over the last half century and this run should continue for a long time.

3. British American Tobacco (symbol BTI—US (adr))* adr is explained below

The second leading tobacco company in the world is British American Tobacco with brands such as Kool, Lucky Strike, Benson & Hedges, and Kent. This company is an American Depositary Receipt (ADR) which means it trades in the US but is actually a foreign company. The idea is that you can buy and sell the ADR which represents shares in the actual company. Although Philip Morris's Marlboro brand is the king of the tobacco brands, British American Tobacco has also done well for shareholders. Here's a quick look at dividend payments.

* Note: Realize the dividends are paid in British Pounds, so the dividend will vary depending on the exchange rate between the Pound and US dollar.

Year	Dividend/Share
2001	$ 0.95
2002	$ 1.16
2003	$ 1.15
2004	$ 1.25
2005	$ 1.35
2006	$ 1.94
2007	$ 2.14
2008	$ 2.63
2009	$ 2.73

Overall smoking is not about to disappear, so both of these companies should continue to print money and raise their dividends for many years into the future.

CHAPTER 9

EAT, DRINK, AND BE WEALTHY

"Ever wonder about those people who spend $2 apiece on those little bottles of Evian water? Try spelling Evian backwards."
—George Carlin

Everybody has to eat and drink! This simple reality has created enormous profits for investors over the years and this is also why there are some great investment opportunities in this area of the stock market. If you look at the best performing stocks over the last number of decades, you will see that food and beverage companies have often been great for shareholders. This is an area where many savvy investors choose to put their money. This is my favourite area to invest in because these companies continue to sell the same products year after year and consumers buy the products and consume them quickly meaning they have to continually keep buying from these companies. I would advise any investor to look closely at this industry. Since the food industry has been such a strong performer over time, I've listed more companies in the list of "idiot-proof" stocks from this industry than any other.

Their Advantage

Food companies benefit from several key advantages. First off, many of these companies control highly respected brands that consumers prefer and are reluctant to do without. The reality is that your mouth is a very personal space and once you've developed a taste for certain types of foods, you continue wanting more of the same and will even have a craving for that specific food item. In addition, once the big companies have created a following for their products, it is very difficult for upstart brands to get shelf space in large grocery stores—success tends to create continued success. In addition, worldwide distribution systems are not easy to build, so companies that have already established their systems have a huge advantage.

Potential Risks

These companies used to be one-decision stocks in the sense that you could simply buy some shares at reasonable prices and then hold onto them for decades— benefiting from ever-increasing profits and collecting ever-rising dividends. However, over the last number of years store brands have become more popular as price-conscious consumers switched away from their regular brands in order to save money. This has had the affect of cutting the sales volume of the national brands while also reducing the companies' ability to increase prices (and profits) on their products.

One of the keys for investors is to look at where the sales of the companies' products occur. The reality when it comes to consumers is that many people will pay $5 for a special cup of their favourite coffee at a trendy coffee shop and then price compare an hour later while they are doing their groceries—and choose one product over another for a 40-cent savings. Generally, the best food companies with the highest profit margins will be ones who have a sizeable percentage of their sales at convenience stores or vending machines. The impulse purchases generally are more profitable for the companies selling the products. Even at grocery stores, look at the companies that have their products right by the cash register. This is fertile ground for high-profit companies.

Some good candidates

1. Coca-Cola (symbol KO—US)

Regarded as the world's most valuable brand, coca-cola is an incredible company. Coca-Cola was first formulated in 1886 by John Pemberton as a medicine but over time its popularity has grown such that it is now sold in over 200 countries around the world. Coke is available in super-markets, convenience stores, fast food restaurants, gas stations, and vending machines all around the world. As a testament to the strength of the brand, go into any store and take a look at the price of Coke compared to the store brands. The products are very similar and have similar costs to produce, but Coke will sell for a substantial premium. Look at the price in vending machines—great profit margins! If you look at the annual report, you will see that the volume of coke is forever growing—especially in emerging markets. For example, per capita consumption in the US is currently 399 beverages per year, while the numbers in China and India are only 30 and 9 drinks per person. As consumption levels rise toward US levels over the coming decades, Coke is destined to make a lot more in profits.

As companies make more profits, they often raise their dividends—and Coca-Cola has been doing that for years. The company has paid uninterrupted dividends since 1893 and has increased its dividend for 47 consecutive years! Here's a snapshot over the last 10 years:

Year	Dividend/Share
2000	$ 0.68
2001	$ 0.72
2002	$ 0.80
2003	$ 0.88
2004	$ 1.00
2005	$ 1.12
2006	$ 1.24
2007	$ 1.36
2008	$ 1.52
2009	$ 1.64

This company has been a great investment over the decades and it should continue to be for decades more.

As a final note on this company, it is important to understand that it has moved well beyond its original iconic brand—Coca-Cola. One thing I have noticed is that the company is really trying to broaden its appeal to various segments of the population. A recent example is the market push behind the newer brand, *Glaceau Vitaminwater*. I have noticed this brand popping up at various recreation centres in unique vending machines and it

seems like a good strategy to capture a part of the market
that is totally missed by offering traditional soft drinks.

2. Pepsico Inc. (symbol PEP—US)

Started in 1898 by Caleb Bradham, Pepsi has grown over
the years to compete with Coca-Cola. In most areas of the
world including the US, Coke outsells Pepsi and
continues to be "the real thing" when it comes to soft
drinks—with Pepsi maintaining its very strong number
two position. Having said that, there are some areas
where Pepsi dominates—such as the sports drink market
with Gatorade. In 2000, Pepsi bought out Quaker Oats
Company and obtained this iconic brand—the number
one sports drink in the world.

Even though Pepsico might only be the #2 drink
company—it is clearly the "king of potato chips" with
various brands such as Ruffles, Lays, Doritos, and many
others. The Quaker Oats acquisition has also been used to
bolster the snack food business by developing different, in
some cases healthier snacks using the highly recognizable
"Quaker Man". Overall, the cola wars are irrelevant—
Pepsi is a great company that generates excellent returns
for shareholders and has managed to raise its dividend
for 38 consecutive years. Here's a quick look at the
dividend history over the last 10 years:

Year	Dividend/Share
2000	$ 0.56
2001	$ 0.58
2002	$ 0.60
2003	$ 0.63
2004	$ 0.85
2005	$ 1.01
2006	$ 1.16
2007	$ 1.43
2008	$ 1.65
2009	$ 1.78

Overall, you should do very well over the long-term owning either Coca-Cola or Pepsico. As countries around the world develop and incomes rise, these companies will earn higher profits.

3. Diageo (symbol DEO—US (adr))

This is a company that you might not have heard of but chances are you've heard of its branded alcoholic drinks. Headquartered in London, England, this company is the result of a merger in 1997 between Guinness plc and Grand Metropolitan plc. Just as I had mentioned Corby in my first book as the largest marketer and manufacturer of spirits in Canada, Diageo is the largest in the entire world. Just as I explained that Corby created rivers of cash for shareholders, the same can be said for Diageo (please read the note at the end of this section about Corby).

At one time Diageo owned unrelated brands such as Pillsbury and Burger King, but over the last number of years they have sold off these businesses to focus on their core business—alcoholic drinks. This focus has allowed them to capture 8 of the world's top 20 premium spirits brands operating in over 180 countries worldwide. These brands included Smirnoff, Baileys, Johnnie Walker, Jose Cuervo, Tanqueray, and Captain Morgan (among others) while the beer portfolio includes Guinness—the best selling stout in the world.

The beauty of the drinks business is that many consumers are brand loyal so they are not very price sensitive and this allows for huge profit margins. In addition, taxes make up a large portion of the purchase price, so small price increases go mostly unnoticed by consumers. BUT, these small price increases add huge amounts of profit to the companies that make the products (similar to the tobacco industry).

It's important to note that Diageo is actually a British company which trades as an ADR (American Depository Receipt) which I explained a little earlier. Here's a quick snapshot of the 10-year dividend history.

* Note: Realize the dividends are paid in British Pounds, so the dividend will vary depending on the exchange rate between the Pound and US dollar.

Year	Dividend/Share
2000	$ 1.25
2001	$ 1.29
2002	$ 1.43
2003	$ 1.67
2004	$ 1.99
2005	$ 2.13
2006	$ 2.26
2007	$ 2.62
2008	$ 2.50
2009	$ 2.27

* Note on Corby Distilleries: In 2005 Pernod Ricard (the world's second-largest spirits maker) gained control of 51% of Corby's voting shares, effectively gaining control of the company. Early in 2006, Corby announced it was selling its interest in the Tia Maria brand in exchange for the distribution rights of the Pernod Ricard brands in Canada for 15 years along with a couple of other assets. Overall, I feel ownership of great brands is much more valuable than merely the "rights to distribute" a brand for a fixed period of time. As a result of this transaction, I've decided that being a shareholder of Corby's was not worth it for me, and I have sold my shares in Corby as a result.

4. Kraft Foods (symbol KFT—US)

It is amazing to note that Kraft products are present in more than 99% of US households. Internationally, Kraft is the second-largest food and drink company in the world. It used to be owned by Philip Morris (tobacco) but was completely spun off a few years ago. This company owns numerous billion dollar brands and has over 40 brands that are more than 100 years old! The one concern many investors would have is that the company's products are sold in supermarkets and this is an area where consumers are very price-conscious. As mentioned earlier, a couple of decades ago, having great brands that consumers flocked to was essentially a license to print money, but over the last number of years things have changed. Stores introduced their own "store brands" such as "No Name" and "President's Choice" at Loblaws, "Great Value" at Wal-Mart, and "Life" brands at Shoppers Drug Mart. These store brands offer good value to customers as they are often of very high quality but at cheaper prices. Think about it. When you are buying cheese, are you loyal only to Kraft cheese or will you buy the store brand if it is cheaper? Many people are not that loyal to these products and therefore profits fall.

So why would I mention Kraft as one of the "idiot-proof stocks" to buy? The reason is that the company is shifting its attention to confectionary products. In early

2010, Kraft acquired Cadbury to become the world's largest confectioner—with products such as Caramilk, Maynards Candies, and Trident Gum. The gum and chocolate bar business is very profitable as these are often impulse buys at a convenience store or gas station. Although people don't have specific brand loyalty to one chocolate bar, they often have four or five favourites that they will purchase regularly. In addition, Kraft is leveraging its Oreo and Ritz brands and using them to create snacks. Finally, Cadbury was a British company with long histories operating in various parts of the world such as India (a former British colony), so this merger will help Kraft in these markets over the long term. I think the company will take a while to integrate its Cadbury acquisition, but over time it should do well for investors. Here's the dividend history since it became an independent company:

Year	Dividend/Share
2002	$ 0.54
2003	$ 0.63
2004	$ 0.75
2005	$ 0.85
2006	$ 0.94
2007	$ 1.02
2008	$ 1.10
2009	$ 1.16

* It should be noted that profits have not climbed like dividends have since the spin-off, so you might want to wait and see how the company performs going forward. It seems with the company's Cadbury acquisition that they will have a great opportunity to bolster profits in the years ahead however.

5. The Hershey Co (symbol HSY—US)

In 1894, a fellow by the name of Milton Hershey decided to use a sweet chocolate coating for his caramels and called his company the Hershey Chocolate Company. Then in 1900, he began using milk chocolate to produce various bars and wafers followed in 1907 with the ever popular Hershey Kiss. Through mass production, Hershey was able to take a luxury product and make it affordable for the masses. Over time the product line grew and in 1956, the H.B. Reese Candy Company was sold to Hershey.

An interesting side note is that in 1918 Milton Hershey transferred the bulk of his wealth including $60 million worth of Hershey stock to The Milton Hershey School Trust—an organization that offers education to under-privileged children. The original gift has grown in value such that the value of the trust's assets now exceeds $6 billion—over 100 times the value of the original gift!

For other shareholders, owning Hershey stock has been almost as enjoyable as tasting the delicious chocolate the company produces. Here's a quick snapshot of the dividends over the past decade:

Year	Dividend/Share
2000	$ 0.54
2001	$ 0.58
2002	$ 0.63
2003	$ 0.73
2004	$ 0.84
2005	$ 0.93
2006	$ 1.05
2007	$ 1.14
2008	$ 1.19
2009	$ 1.19
2010	(projected) $ 1.28

I like snack foods as an investment because people are often loyal certain brands. People generally don't buy generic chocolate bars. This company should continue to reward investors over time.

Once again, look for companies that generate a large portion of their sales from vending machines or convenience stores—so they will be able to keep fat profit margins over time. Now let's take a look at distributors of food as other possible investment candidates...

Not only are branded food companies a great place to look for solid long-term investments—many companies that deliver food to you have also been good investments over time. The reality is that restaurants litter the landscape of most major cities, but many of the restaurants are chains or franchises controlled by huge corporations. Having said all that, the restaurant industry is very competitive with generally low profit margins. There can be trendy brands that appear once in a while and then fizzle a few years later. In order to reduce your risk, I would stick with brands of restaurants that have been around a long time...

1. McDonald's Corp (symbol MCD—US)

As I have 5 kids, I have spent an incredible amount of time at various McDonald's over the last number of years. The assembly-line concept so common in fast food restaurants today was originally created by two brothers—Richard and Maurice McDonald. They originally called this production approach the "Speedee Service System". Then in 1954, a milkshake machine salesman by the name of Ray Kroc learned that the brothers were using 8 of his milkshake machines at their restaurant (which was a large volume in those days) and he had to see the restaurant for himself. He was so impressed with the restaurant that he told the brothers they should franchise the system. When the brothers hesitated, Kroc volunteered to do it for them and he returned home with the rights to franchise the McDonald's system across the US (with the exception of a few small territories). Over time Kroc was often frustrated with the McDonald brothers, so he bought out control of McDonald's in 1961.

It's a little-known fact that although McDonald's has made a fortune by selling hamburgers, Kroc's meeting with Harry Sonnenborne created the model Kroc used to make an even bigger fortune. Sonneborne created a plan whereby Kroc would create a company that would buy land or lease all the land on which McDonald's restaurants would be built. Franchisees would then rent the land from Kroc's company and Kroc would earn the greater of rent or a percentage of the franchisees' sales. Today McDonald's owns an incredible amount of commercial land in prime locations around the world—it has approximately 31,000 locations across the globe at last count.

Regardless of what you might think of the food, McDonald's has been absolutely yummy for investors. On Wikipedia, it mentions that if you had purchased 100 shares when they first became public in 1965, they would have cost you a little more than $2,000, but they would now be worth over $4 million! Here's a quick snapshot of the 10-year dividend history:

Year	Dividend/Share
2000	$ 0.22
2001	$ 0.23
2002	$ 0.24
2003	$ 0.40
2004	$ 0.55
2005	$ 0.67
2006	$ 1.00
2007	$ 1.50
2008	$ 1.63
2009	$ 2.05

I noticed a lot of McDonald's restaurants when I lived in Asia and I would imagine more will be built as countries develop over time. Note that there are other restaurant companies you could invest in, but there are no other restaurant companies with the size and brand recognition of McDonald's.

2. Sysco (symbol SYY—US)

Sysco might not be a company that you have heard of but if you eat food away from home, you have definitely consumed products distributed by Sysco. This company is the leading distributor of food, equipment, and supplies to the US foodservice industry. This is a low-margin business with extremely high fixed costs for warehouses, trucks and other equipment—so what would make Sysco a good investment? It is by far the largest competitor in a highly-fragmented industry which means it is in the position to wring costs out of the system (similar to Wal-Mart in retailing). As such, Sysco has been a great creator of wealth for investors—and more to come as the industry consolidates over the next number of years.

I have a personal affinity for this stock as it became public the same year I was born—1970. During that time it has managed to increase its dividend every year. Here's a quick look at the last 10 years of dividend payments:

Year	Dividend/Share
2000	$ 0.23
2001	$ 0.28
2002	$ 0.36
2003	$ 0.40
2004	$ 0.48
2005	$ 0.56
2006	$ 0.66
2007	$ 0.72
2008	$ 0.82
2009	$ 0.93

As the company continues to grow, shareholders should continue to collect generous dividends. The only reservation I would have about Sysco is that it is overwhelmingly focused on North America so you are getting very little exposure to international markets with this company. However with the US population expected to increase by 100 million people over the next few decades along with the continued consolidation of this industry, I have voted with my wallet and am happy to own some shares of this wonderful business.

3. Tim Horton's (symbol THI-Canada)

Started in 1964 by hockey player Tim Horton and his partner Jim Charade, this doughnut chain has grown to become the largest restaurant chain in Canada with over 3,000 locations in its home market—not to mention another 500-plus locations in the US. Tim Hortons owns a commanding 76% market share for baked goods in Canada and you can see long line-ups every morning as Canadians wait to buy their morning coffee.

This company was bought by Wendy's (the hamburger chain) in 1995, but became a stand-alone company again in 2006. At the time Tim Hortons went public, the stock was very expensive compared to earnings, but over the last few years the share price has not increased very much while earnings have doubled—making the stock more reasonably priced. This is one of the rare Canadian companies that has successfully expanded into the US market

—albeit at a slow pace. Here's a quick look at the dividends since the company became public again in 2006:

Year	Dividend/Share
2006	$ 0.14
2007	$ 0.28
2008	$ 0.36
2009	$ 0.40
2010	(projected) $ 0.52

The simple reality is that coffee and sugar products are addictive, cheap, and profitable so if you buy this stock at a reasonable price, it should generate wealth for you over time. By buying shares in Timmy's, next time you're waiting in the typical long line-up for your coffee and Timbits, you can pass the time watching the money being raked in and think of how some of that money will be coming back to you as a shareholder.

4. Starbuck's (symbol **SBUX**—US)

Since coffee is addictive and cheap to produce, this company is well-positioned to make money. Starbuck's has managed to get consumers to fork over $4 or more for a specially prepared coffee and it has grown immensely over the years—opening locations across the globe.

I first stumbled upon Starbuck's in the mid 1990s when I moved to Vancouver. Upon seeing Starbuck's on virtually every street corner, I research this company and bought shares. These shares have gone up almost 1,000% since then. Unfortunately, I managed to snatch defeat from the jaws of investing victory and sold the shares shortly after I had purchased them for a quick 20% gain. This is one of the more idiotic aspects of my investment career, which leads me to an important fact:

I have lost A LOT MORE money selling stocks that I should have kept than buying stocks I shouldn't have. If you buy quality, don't be an idiot—KEEP THEM!

Over the years Starbuck's has grown to become the largest coffee retailer in the world. I wrote an article in *Canadian MoneySaver* in 2008 explaining what I liked about Starbucks. I liked the idea that they were continually reinvesting their profits into new store openings and predicted they would pay a dividend at some future date. Since that time they have grown from 13,000 to over 16,000 stores within their system. They also initiated a dividend in early 2010.

The nice thing about coffee is that it is consumed worldwide but in most cases small "mom and pop" coffee shops service the addiction of caffeine addicts. If coffee follows the same path as the restaurant industry has over the last few decades, there is still a lot of consolidation to occur—which will be great for Starbuck's.

* Note: Up until quite recently, Starbuck's reinvested all its profits into its business, but recently it started paying dividends. It started with a 10 cent dividend, and then increased that 30% in its next dividend payment. I would bet that over time Starbuck's will reward shareholders with many increasing dividends but if you want to be very conservative, you might want to wait to see a more established track record of dividends.

CHAPTER 10

SHOPPING FOR MONEY

"We used to build civilizations.
Now we build shopping malls."
—Bill Bryson

Generally speaking, retailing is a very competitive industry. History is littered with former superstar retailers that
were not able to adapt to changes that occurred and went
out of business. The trouble with retailing is that customers can essentially "walk across the street" if they don't
like your offerings or prices. I would also avoid "trendy"
retailers like the plague. These companies appear
seemingly overnight offering a new product (usually
clothing) and then disappear almost as quickly as the
appeared. In addition, even retailers offering necessities
can have their customers taken away from them if they

make some wrong moves. Having said all this, there are still a few companies that I would consider investing in that have strong competitive advantages.

Their Advantage

Many retailers automatically get a lot of customer traffic so they have a captive market within their stores. Super-efficient retailers such as Wal-Mart can offer very competitive prices and keep customers coming back week after week. Retailers that can build up relationships with customers such as the relationship you might have with your pharmacist can also create constant store traffic and create sales . In addition, they can use this customer traffic to create their own store brands which helps generate more profit and also helps build brand loyalty.

Potential Risks

Once again… consumers are generally not very loyal. If a competitor can offer something another store can't (such as lower prices), that store will lose customers very quickly.

　　1.　Wal-Mart (symbol WMT—US)

At the age of 26, Sam Walton began managing a variety store in Newport, Arkansas. This was in 1945—immediately after WWII. There he pioneered many retailing concepts that would later catapult him into the ranks of the super-wealthy. In 1962 he opened his first store in Arkansas and gradually expanded from there. He was obsessed with offering customers the lowest possible prices on a wide variety of merchandise. In personal interviews, his family has mentioned that Walton was obsessed with K-mart early on—so much so that he could not drive past a K-mart without stopping in and looking at how they were doing things. It's interesting to note that K-mart opened its first store in 1962—the same year the first Wal-Mart store came into existence. Like the "Hare" from the Aesop fable *"The Tortoise and the Hare"*, K-mart grew much more quickly than Wal-Mart over the first number of years of their existence. But just as in the story, the Tortoise (Wal-Mart) continued to plod along and eventually overtook K-Mart. In fact Wal-Mart became so successful that K-mart had to seek Chapter 11 bankruptcy protection in 2002. Here in Canada, K-mart was ubiquitous when I was a child, but it no longer exists.

Today Wal-Mart is very difficult to compete with. Its massive scale and efficiency allows it to offer good prices on a wide range of goods and it continues to churn out ever-increasing profits year after year. As an illustration of just how much wealth this company has generated, it's interesting to note that if founder Sam Walton were still alive today, his net worth would dwarf that of even Bill

Gates as his family fortune now amounts to around $90 billion (compared to Gates's $50 billion). This company has managed 35 consecutive years of dividend increases. Here's a snapshot of the last 10 years:

Year	Dividend/Share
2000	$ 0.23
2001	$ 0.27
2002	$ 0.30
2003	$ 0.35
2004	$ 0.48
2005	$ 0.58
2006	$ 0.65
2007	$ 0.83
2008	$ 0.93
2009	$ 1.06

2. Shoppers Drug Mart (symbol SC—CAN)

I go to Shopper's Drug Mart on a daily basis to mail my books at the post office. I can see that this store is always busy. Murry Koffler inherited two pharmacies at the age of 20 and gradually grew the chain to 17 stores before renaming them "Shoppers Drug Mart" in 1962. Koffler insisted his pharmacists wear starched white coats as a sign that they were medical professionals. He later

pioneered the idea of franchising the stores to the pharmacists so that they would own the stores and share in the
profits. After Koffler retired, he sold Shopper's Drug Mart
to Imasco—an ironic twist considering Imasco was
formerly Imperial Tobacco—Canada's largest tobacco
company at that time. Eventually Shoppers was spun off
and sold to the public where it now operates over 1,000
stores across the country.

As I've mentioned, retailing is a competitive industry
because your customers have very little loyalty to you. If
a competitor offers a better deal, customers will leave at
the drop of a hat. The competitive advantage Wal-Mart
has is that it can offer great prices on most items because
of its scale. Although Shoppers also benefits from scale in
the pharmacy industry, it is in a slightly different position
than that of an average retailer because over time many
people build up a relationship with their pharmacist as a
partner in their medical care. This relationship allows the
pharmacist to know if one medication might interfere
with another—and alert their customer. This fact encou-
rages customers to have a little more loyalty to the
pharmacist and not look at their relationship solely based
on price. In addition, many people have drug plans so a lot
of the costs do not come directly out of their own pocket—
also encouraging them to be a little less price-sensitive.

The demographic picture is bright for Shoppers

because as the boomers age, they will need more medication and Shoppers is in a great position to fill that need. In addition, there are many independent "mom and pop" pharmacies across the country and over time the industry will consolidate (as happens over time with virtually every industry). This means Shopper's is in a sweet spot where it can be the consolidator—just as the fast food brands consolidated the restaurant industry during the 1970s and 80s. Here is a quick snapshot of the dividends since the company started paying them in 2005:

Year	Dividend/Share
2005	$ 0.40
2006	$ 0.48
2007	$ 0.64
2008	$ 0.86
2009	$ 0.86
2010	(projected) $ 0.90

CHAPTER 11

AROUND THE HOUSE— "CLEANING UP!"

"Cleaning anything involves making something else dirty, but anything can get dirty without something else getting clean."
—**Laurence Peter**

Many people are loyal to certain brands found around the house—whether it be Sunlight dish soap or Colgate toothpaste. These brands are used regularly and are trusted by many consumers.

Their Advantage

Many of the brands offered by these companies have been around for generations and are trusted by consumers. In addition, since these companies have been operating for so long they have built up many needed brands that stores simply have to carry or else they'll lose sales. With the sheer scale of many of these companies, they can negotiate good pricing and monopolize premium shelf space in stores—which squeezes out any potential competitors.

Potential Risks

Even though these companies own many trusted brands, over the last number of years consumers have realized that many store brands can be equally as good as the ones these companies offer. Products you don't ingest (such as food or drinks) often do not create the same degree of brand loyalty because you don't develop a taste (or craving) for them—you simply buy the products you feel are best. As a result, these companies can face threats from cheaper offerings from retailers.

1. Proctor and Gamble (symbol PG—US)

If you've ever used Tide laundry detergent, Folgers coffee, Pampers diapers, Gillette razors, Duracell batteries, or a host of other products, then you've enriched the coffers of The Proctor and Gamble Company. Founded over 150 years ago in 1837 by William Proctor and James Gamble, the company was originally in the business of selling candles. Then a strange thing happened in 1879 when a soap maker went to lunch and forgot to turn off the soap mixer. The result was that more than the normal amount of air was added to the batch. Since the soap maker did not want to face the possible consequences of his actions, he secretly packaged and shipped the soap. Soon customers from everywhere were requesting more of the "soap that floats" and the brand, Ivory Soap was born.

Today people around the world use P&G brands over 3 billion times a day. The company owns no less than 23 billion-dollar brands worldwide and it generates more than half its sales overseas. Even though many of its products will face stiff competition from various store brands, it is one giant company that can negotiate on equal footing with retailing behemoths such as Wal-Mart. The simple reality is that any retailer who wants to be taken seriously *has to* do business with P&G. In addition, the company's products are used in good times and bad— so the company offers very steady performance. Over time, its overseas sales should continue to grow as emerging market consumers demand quality brands.

This company is an eminent dividend-payer and has been paying *uninterrupted dividends since 1890!* In addition, the company has been increasing its dividend for 53 straight years. Here's a quick snapshot of the last ten years:

Year	Dividend/Share
2000	$ 0.64
2001	$ 0.70
2002	$ 0.76
2003	$ 0.82
2004	$ 0.93
2005	$ 1.03
2006	$ 1.15
2007	$ 1.28
2008	$ 1.45
2009	$ 1.64

2. Colgate-Palmolive (symbol CL—US)

If there was a "little brother" of Proctor and Gamble, it would definitely be Colgate-Palmolive. Where P&G makes Crest toothpaste, Colgate-Palmolive obviously makes Colgate. This company offers Irish Spring soap versus Ivory....and the list of similar products goes on. An interesting difference is that Colgate generates a much larger percentage of its sales overseas than P&G (more than 75%). If you feel that the emerging markets are the place to make money over the coming years, then Colgate-Palmolive is a good way to do it.

It's interesting to note that Colgate has actually been around for over 200 years—since 1806. Started in New

York by William Colgate, the company operates in over 200 countries today. This company has managed to reward investors with uninterrupted dividends since 1895 and it has also increased those dividends for 47 consecutive years. Here's a quick snapshot of the last ten years:

Year	Dividend/Share
2000	$ 0.63
2001	$ 0.68
2002	$ 0.72
2003	$ 0.90
2004	$ 0.96
2005	$ 1.11
2006	$ 1.25
2007	$ 1.40
2008	$ 1.56
2009	$ 1.72

3. Unilever (symbol UL—US (ADR))

Touching the lives of over 2 billion people a day, Unilever produces a wide variety of food, personal care and household brands. Included in its portfolio of food brands are such well-known names as Lipton, Knorr, Slim-Fast and Breyer's among others. In personal care, Unilver offers commonly found items such as Dove soap and

Vaseline. Around the house, you can also find names such as Sunlight and Vim. If you look around your house, odds are you have at least a few brands from Unilever. This stock trades as an American Depository Receipt in the US.

* Note: Realize the dividends are paid in foreign currency, so the dividend will vary depending on the exchange rate of the US dollar.

Here's a quick snapshot of the 10-year dividend history:

Year	Dividend/Share
2000	$ 0.96
2001	$ 0.95
2002	$ 1.31
2003	$ 1.92
2004	$ 1.69
2005	$ 1.36
2006	$ 1.44
2007	$ 1.75
2008	$ 2.54
2009	$ 1.68
2010	(projected) $ 2.10

CHAPTER 12

HEALTH MAKES WEALTH!

"Expensive medicines are always good:
if not for the patient, at least for the druggist"
—**Russian Proverb**

From the list of top performing stocks at the beginning of this book, you will notice that many of the best-performing stocks from 1957-2003 were pharmaceutical stocks. These companies benefited from having many trusted over-the-counter medicine as well as many patented prescription drugs which generated huge profits. If a company can develop a great product and get a patent for it—profit margins can be huge. However, over the last number of years, many generic drug companies have increased competition such that as soon as patents expire, they quickly begin to sell generic equivalents—which reduce the profits from the big pharmaceutical companies. Many large pharmaceutical companies will probably continue to be huge money-makers, but there will be risks.

Regardless of the risks, the simple reality is that in the developed world the baby boomers are aging and will consume more health care over the next few decades. In addition, people in the developing world are living longer, getting wealthier, and demanding better health care products. These factors bode well for this industry in general.

Their Advantage

When people are dealing with their health, they are not price-sensitive. They will generally choose products they trust—even if they cost a little more. This is one of the reasons over-the-counter branded drugs can charge a premium for their products over the generic variety. Many large companies are similar in this respect to branded food companies. With medical devices, surgeons get used to certain products and develop a preference for them. The reality is that switching surgical products is often trickier than simply popping a different pill in your mouth. This reality creates a little more loyalty to certain products. In addition, with medical devices, the ultimate consumer does not make the decision on which product to use—this is often done by the surgeon or other third-parties.

Potential Risks

This is a very competitive industry with new products being introduced regularly which might be better than existing products. In addition, this industry can be exposed to potential lawsuits as some drugs end up creating unforeseen side-effects in some people.

Overall, there are a lot of good candidates operating in this area, but I've chosen a few that I am most familiar with.

1. Johnson and Johnson (symbol JNJ—US)

This is one of my all-time favourite companies and I have written about it a number of times. J&J has helped create wealth for many investors over the years and there is no reason to expect that to change in the future. This is by far one of the most diversified health care companies in the world with three large business segments: Pharmaceuticals, Consumer Products, and Medical Devices. If you agree that health care is a good area to invest in, than J&J covers a lot of different areas under one umbrella.

Founded in 1886, this company has been touted as one of the world's "most respected companies" a number of times and is one of only a handful of companies with a AAA financial credit rating (meaning it is financially very stable). This stock is a proverbial "Rock of Gibraltar" and has made many investors wealthy over the years. It has managed to pay 46 consecutive years of increasing dividends. Here's a quick look at the last 10 years:

Year	Dividend/Share
2000	$ 0.62
2001	$ 0.70
2002	$ 0.80
2003	$ 0.92
2004	$ 1.10
2005	$ 1.28
2006	$ 1.46
2007	$ 1.62
2008	$ 1.80
2009	$ 1.93

2. Becton, Dickinson (symbol BDX—US)

This company manufactures medical devices, diagnostic equipment, and produces research and clinical tools for biosciences. Started in 1897, the company has grown to become a medical giant valued at over $16 billion. The company shares went public in 1962, and 10 shares purchased at that time would now have grown to 1,150 shares. You can see "BD" products throughout hospitals. The company is a steady earnings-grower and dividend-payer with dividends being paid since 1926. Becton,

Dickinson has also increased its dividend for 37 straight years. Here's a quick look at the last 10 years:

Year	Dividend/Share
2000	$ 0.37
2001	$ 0.38
2002	$ 0.39
2003	$ 0.40
2004	$ 0.60
2005	$ 0.72
2006	$ 0.86
2007	$ 0.98
2008	$ 1.14
2009	$ 1.32

3. C.R. Bard (symbol BCR—US)

Started by Charles Russell Bard in the early 1900s, CR Bard began distributing a urethral catheter in 1907. Over the next 100-plus years, Bard grew incredibly. Today the company is a multi-billion dollar medical company with operations in many different countries. This company is still relatively small compared to some of the other publicly traded companies, but is has managed to pay increasing dividends for 39 straight years. However it's important to realize that most of its profits are reinvested to grow its business over time—and this strategy has led to pretty impressive growth for investors. Regardless, here's a quick look at the dividend payments over the last 10 years:

Year	Dividend/Share
2000	$ 0.41
2001	$ 0.42
2002	$ 0.43
2003	$ 0.45
2004	$ 0.47
2005	$ 0.50
2006	$ 0.54
2007	$ 0.58
2008	$ 0.62
2009	$ 0.66

CHAPTER 13

OILY RIVERS OF PROFITS

"My formula for success is rise early, work late, and strike oil."
—J. Paul Getty

The oil and gas industry can be a great industry that generates great wealth for many investors. John D. Rockefeller used his oil company to become the richest man in the world during his time. Today, oil exporting countries can generate huge wealth. Oil and natural gas are the lifeblood of the modern economy and will be for the foreseeable future.

Here in Canada, we are very fortunate that we have been endowed with an abundance of oil and natural gas. There are numerous great investment opportunities in the Canadian oil and gas sector, but now I prefer to stick with the largest vertically integrated companies which reduces the downside risk somewhat. This is slightly different than my view a few years ago, so let's take a moment to look at my thinking on this...

A number of years ago (in the early 2000s) when oil was trading below $30 per barrel, there was a tremendous opportunity for investors to make a lot of money investing in oil producing companies that had the ability to increase production dramatically. Some of these companies were high cost producers—but this meant that they would profit more than low cost producers if oil prices rose. Let me use a fictional example to explain.

Suppose oil sells for $25 per barrel and Company A produces oil for a cost of $5 per barrel while Company B must pay $20 to produce a barrel of oil. So right now their **profit per barrel of oil is:**

Company A:

$25 price per barrel – $5 cost per barrel = $20 profit per barrel

Company B:

$25 price per barrel – $20 cost per barrel = $5 profit per barrel

Now let's assume there is a big run-up in price (like we've witnessed over the last number of years). If we assume that oil prices double to $50 per barrel, the new profit per barrel for each company would be:

Company A:

$50 price per barrel – $5 cost per barrel = $45 profit per barrel

Company B:

$50 price per barrel – $20 cost per barrel = $30 profit per barrel

In the case of:

Company A: Its profits rise ($45 divided by $20) = **125%**

BUT Company B's profits rise ($30 divided by $5) = **600%**

Look at the difference!

The net result is that companies that are high-cost produces end up doing much better when oil prices rise than low-cost producers. In addition, in this environment, integrated oil companies (the companies that also transport, refine, and market gas through gas stations) do not see their profits rise as much as straight oil producers.

It is because of these factors that I've changed strategies with oil and gas. When I first invested in oil stocks, NOBODY was talking about oil—so the shares were cheap. Now it seems there is a new announcement every week talking about how expensive oil is going to be and how we are going to run out. This talk has caused oil stocks to become much more expensive than they were a few years ago. Realizing that I am an idiot investor who has no clue about the future, I've decided to stick with integrated oil companies because even though they don't gain as much when oil prices rise meteorically, they also don't get crushed when oil prices fall precipitously (and they do okay with stagnant oil prices). With all this in mind, here are a couple of companies that can do okay over the long term in both good and bad oil markets:

1. Imperial Oil (symbol IMO—CAN)

Founded in 1880 in London, Ontario, Imperial Oil is the largest integrated oil company in Canada. It operates a retail network of Esso gas stations in addition to refineries and other related businesses. Over time it has expanded production in the Oil Sands through partial ownership in Syncrude in addition to other wholly owned projects.

This is a company I mentioned in my second book, *The Lazy Investor*. Over time it has paid off debt such that today it is virtually debt-free and it carries a triple 'A' credit rating (a rating reserved for only the most conservative companies). Oil and natural gas are the lifeblood of our modern economy and as long as that remains true, Imperial Oil will continue to make money.

One interesting fact about this company is that it buys back a tremendous amount of shares every year. This has the effect of gradually reducing the total number of shares outstanding which means that investors gradually own a larger piece of this great company. The company has bought back half of its outstanding shares since 1995. *This company prefers to give money back to shareholders by buying back its shares.* This approach has a similar effect as DRIPping (as I explained in *The Lazy Investor*). However, it has also increased its dividend for many years. Here's a quick look:

Year	Dividend/Share
2000	$ 0.26
2001	$ 0.27
2002	$ 0.28
2003	$ 0.29
2004	$ 0.29
2005	$ 0.31
2006	$ 0.32
2007	$ 0.35
2008	$ 0.38
2009	$ 0.40
2010	(projected) $ 0.43

Realize that there are a number of good oil and gas investments you can choose in Canada and Imperial Oil is one of the great companies to consider.

2. ExxonMobil

It seems strange to hold a US oil company when oil and gas is one of the largest industries in Canada, but I was able to buy shares fairly cheaply, so I am happy to own a part of this huge company.

Exxon was originally part of John D. Rockefeller's Standard Oil Trust. It merged with Mobil in 1999 to create the largest oil behemoth in the world. Today it operates in numerous countries around the world. It continually breaks all-time profit records for US corporations and is seen as a very conservatively managed company—one of only a handful of companies with a coveted 'AAA' financial rating. In addition to this, a huge portion of the profits earned by this company occur outside the US.

Exxon has managed to pay out dividends for around 100 years and has also increased its dividend every year for decades. BUT the real story lies in what it's been doing with the rest of its cash. A quick look at the most recent annual report shows some interesting facts in "Statement of Cash Flows". In this statement you can see that Exxon spent around $8 billion for shareholder dividends (the money you passively receive every quarter) and another $19 billion in buying back shares during the most recent year. In the previous year it spent around $8 billion in dividends and a full $35 billion in share buybacks. Share buybacks are the most efficient method for a company to give money to shareholders because they don't have to pay tax on it as they do with dividends, but over time share buybacks add value. In a downturn, there are very few oil companies that will do as well as ExxonMobil, and

I'm happy to sit back and collect the ever-rising dividends. Here's a quick look at the last 10 years of dividend payments:

YearDividend/Share	
2000	$ 0.88
2001	$ 0.91
2002	$ 0.92
2003	$ 0.98
2004	$ 1.06
2005	$ 1.14
2006	$ 1.28
2007	$ 1.37
2008	$ 1.55
2009	$ 1.66
2010	(projected) $ 1.74

This is one of the lowest-risk companies within the oil and gas industry.

CHAPTER 14

ENTERTAIN, COMMUNICATE, AND ENRICH!

"Television is like the toaster, you push a button and the same thing pops up every time."
—Alfred Hitchcock

Entertainment is an industry that benefits greatly as countries become more affluent. However in most cases its offerings are not recession-proof products, so that makes me cautious. In addition, I am not really all that sure how new technology will affect this industry. Twenty years ago the newspaper industry was essentially a license to print money as it was one of the only means to connect people and advertise products. The reality is that the internet has changed all that. Today, many newspapers are struggling and some have gone out of business—so this is an area where I would tread carefully. Having said all that, I would feel comfortable owning the company that provides the *access* to the internet, TV, or mobile phones.

The Advantage

Similar to pipelines in the fact that it costs billions of dollars to build up the infrastructure needed to offer cable TV or telephone services, this industry is a cash machine once the infrastructure has been built. This is because new entrants have to invest enormous sums of money with little chance of making profits against the established companies—and this fact keeps the competition away for the most part...which keeps profits up.

Potential Risks

These companies face the risk that new technology could change their profitability. Think back a couple of decades and dominant telephone companies were practically money printing machines with their telephone networks and enormous long-distance charges. These factors have been destroyed through technology as regular telephones are in slow decline and long distance costs have plummeted. I have no clue what technology might appear on the horizon, but the long-term future is not totally clear.

1. Rogers Communication (RCI.b—CAN)

Back in 1960, Ted Rogers bought a struggling radio station and turned it into a success. He followed that up in 1967 with the founding of Rogers Cable TV and formally entered the cable business with 300 subscribers. Gradually over time the company grew and today it has over 2.3 million basic cable, 1.4 million digital cable, 1.5 million internet and 1 million digital phone subscribers. Rogers wireless has 7.4 million subscribers in total. The beauty of this business is that people automatically pay their bills every month, so the money flows to the company regularly. The other benefit is that the costs to set up the networks are huge, but once they are totally set up, each extra subscriber is almost pure profit. Once you reach a critical mass, the business model is very profitable—and Rogers is the largest operator in this space.

The company used to be a debt-laden growth story with meagre profits, but today it generates tremendous cash and can afford to buy various assets such as the SkyDome in Toronto (since renamed the "Rogers Centre"), the CityTV assets and numerous radio stations. In 2007, Rogers attained "investment grade" status for its debt signalling a new maturity for the company. So even though the company does not have a glorious dividend-paying past, it has been growing its payout since it attained investment grade status:

Year	Dividend/Share
2007	$ 0.41
2008	$ 1.00
2009	$ 1.16
2010	(projected) $ 1.28

* Note: Telus and BCE are also large players in telephone, satellite, and wireless (cell phones) and they are worth a look (offering reasonable dividends).

CHAPTER 15

MOVIN' ALONG...
AND MOVIN' ON UP!

"I know I was going to take the wrong train, so I left early."

—Yogi Berra

Generally transportation companies are not an area I would invest in. Airlines have generally been terrible investments over the years—needing huge amounts of money for capital (such as airplanes) while being very dependent on the economy for their business. In addition, they basically sell a commodity product where many airlines compete based on price—so that keeps profits razor-thin (during the years they are able to make a profit).

Having said all that, there is one area of transportation that is appealing—railroads.

Advantages

Why would this capital-intensive industry be a good investment? Think about it. Once the track is laid, no other competitors can build track. With modern cities already built and new environmental laws in place, it would be virtually impossible for a new competitor to arrive on the scene (in contrast to trucking which can have new entrants all the time). In addition, with modern computer guidance and double-stacked cars, rail is the cheapest method for shipping many products. This allows railways to raise prices and still be cheaper than the alternative. Finally, railroads will benefit greatly as trade with new markets (such as China and India) grow over the coming decades. Canada has many resources that the world needs and most of these resources will be shipped by rail because it is the most cost-effective option.

Potential Risks

The very nature of the railway business is that it is cyclical. Although I think trade with Asia (and other parts of the world) will grow in the coming decades, there will be times during economic downturns when railways' profits will decline.

All railroad companies benefit from the advantages I've mentioned, but I would prefer to invest in the best-managed companies and in this case that would be Canadian National Railway.

1. Canadian National Railway (symbol CNR—CAN)

In response to public concerns about losing their transportation links, the Canadian government took control of the nearly bankrupt CNR in 1918 and cobbled it together with a few other failing railways. This public ownership lasted until 1995 when the government sold shares of the company to the public. Since that time CN has made tremendous strides and has become one of the best-run railroads in North America. Today CN owns over 20,000 miles of track stretching from the Atlantic to Pacific to the Gulf of Mexico. As world trade increases this company benefits as virtually everything Canada exports has to be shipped and railways are extensively used.

This is a fertile environment for increased profits (and dividends). Here's a quick snapshot of the last 10 years of dividend payments:

Year	Dividend/Share
2000	$ 0.23
2001	$ 0.26
2002	$ 0.29
2003	$ 0.33
2004	$ 0.39
2005	$ 0.48
2006	$ 0.65
2007	$ 0.84
2008	$ 0.92
2009	$ 1.01
2010	(projected) $ 1.08

This company offers an indirect way to invest in worldwide economic growth that will occur over the coming decades.

THE BUSINESS OF BUSINESS...IS BUSINESS!

"Corporation: an ingenious device for obtaining profit without individual responsibility."
—**Ambrose Bierce**

This is one area of investing that many people overlook because they often don't deal with business services companies in their daily lives. These companies seem BORING to you, however, some of these companies make great profits so let's have a look at a few of them:

Their Advantage

The advantage of these companies is that once they are integrated into their customers' businesses, it becomes too complicated and time-consuming for their customers to switch to their competitors—which often means great profits for these companies.

Possible Risks

Since these companies offer services to business, they often face profit pressure during recessions as companies need less of the services they offer.

Here are a few companies that I like in this area:

1. Automatic Data Processing (symbol ADP—US)

ADP is the largest payroll and tax filing processor in the US with over 585,000 corporate customers. This company provides outsourcing solutions so that corporations can focus more on their business rather than administrative aspects such as payroll and tax filing.

This seemingly boring company has managed to earn steadily increasing profits over the years and has rewarded shareholders with over 30 years of consecutive dividend increases. Here's a quick look at the last 10 years:

Year	Dividend/Share
2000	$ 0.34
2001	$ 0.40
2002	$ 0.45
2003	$ 0.48
2004	$ 0.54
2005	$ 0.61
2006	$ 0.68
2007	$ 0.83
2008	$ 1.04
2009	$ 1.24

One interesting fact about ADP is that they hold money in cash for their corporate clients before it is paid out to employees. As such, a portion of their income is earned from interest on the funds they keep for a short time before it is paid out. So while rising interest rates negatively affect many companies, they actually benefit ADP as the company earns more interest on the money it is holding. This company serves mostly large companies, while another company called Paychex (symbol PAYX—US) serves smaller companies—but both of these companies are debt-free and have similar business models.

2. Dun and Bradstreet (symbol DNB—US)

Founded in 1841 in New York City, D&B provides credit information on businesses and corporations. Currently it keeps track of over 150 million businesses worldwide. This might not sound very exciting, but if companies want to do business such as renting a building or getting suppliers, they often have to pay a fee to Dun and Bradstreet so that they can get a DUNS number to show their creditworthiness. D&B has a huge database of these companies—a database that would be next to impossible to replicate. As such D&B makes great profits.

Since it became a stand-alone company in late 2000, it has managed to buy back almost 40% of its outstanding shares. It started paying dividends in 2007, so here's the brief history:

Year	Dividend/Share
2007	$ 1.00
2008	$ 1.20
2009	$ 1.36
2010	(projected) $ 1.40

This company requires little capital to earn large profits and it's very difficult for competitors to move in—so it makes a good stock to own.

CHAPTER 17

EDU-CASH-IN!

"If you are planning for a year, sow rice; if you are planning for a decade, plant trees; if you are planning for a lifetime, educate people."
—Chinese Proverb

Anyone who has paid their way through university (or paid their kids' way), know firsthand that education is not cheap. Tuition increases are normal—and these increases are usually much higher than general inflation. Many students work very hard in order to pay for their education because of the future benefits it brings.

But wouldn't it be nice to own the university that collects all those tuition fees? In Canada this is difficult, but in the US there are numerous for-profit educational institutions.

Their Advantage

The general trend over time is that you need continually more qualifications in order to begin a good career. Students tend to look for their education not based on price –but on what their desired education will get them. As a result of this, the education industry in the US is very profitable. In addition, certain schools have accreditation (which means that students can transfer their credits to public universities). This is a huge benefit to students so those schools that have accreditation do not have to compete with schools that don't. This means they can raise their prices regularly and earn enormous profits. Obtaining accreditation is extremely difficult, so this advantage is huge.

Possible Risks

The major risk with these companies surfaced around the time of writing this book. The government in the US is thinking about cutting student loans to students of for-profit universities if repayment rates are too low. This would be a major blow to these companies, but to cope they can adjust their costs fairly quickly. If you are conservative, you might want to wait until the final legislation is passed.

1. Strayer Education (symbol STRA—US)

Strayer Education owns Strayer University which has an enrolment of over 50,000 students and offers various degree programs. Overall there are over 75 campuses (with new campuses being added yearly) and also Strayer Online where students can take courses over the internet. This company earns huge profits and is totally debt-free. During economic downturns, enrolment increases as students choose to get more education to compete in the job market. Along with earnings growth of almost 20% per year over the last decade, this company has increased dividends almost 10-fold. Here's the 10-year snapshot:

Year	Dividend/Share
2000	$ 0.25
2001	$ 0.26
2002	$ 0.26
2003	$0.26
2004	$0.41
2005	$0.63
2006	$1.06
2007	$1.31
2008	$1.63
2009	$ 2.25
2010	(projected) $ 3.00

There are other companies worth a look in this area but Strayer is one of the best-managed education stocks available and that's why I've listed it here.

CHAPTER 18

UGLY DUCKLINGS OR BEAUTIFUL SWANS?

*"Go for a business that any idiot can run—
because sooner or later, any idiot probably
is going to run it."*
—**Peter Lynch**

1. C.H. Robinson (symbol CHRW—US)

This is a third-party logistic service company. Essentially, it transports goods using third-party trucks, planes, ships, and railcars. The beauty of this business model is that CH Robinson does not have to invest in expensive equipment. It merely contracts space from a variety of providers (trucks, ships, planes, etc) and then offers that space to the appropriate buyers who want to ship merchandise.

The other big advantage is if shipping volumes fall during economic downturns, the company can quickly reduce its contracted space and it does not get stuck with a lot of (expensive) idle trucks waiting to deliver goods.

The company makes loads of money and is totally debt-free as it does not have to buy the expensive vehicles to ship goods. Here's a quick snapshot of its 10-year dividend history:

Year	Dividend/Share
2000	$ 0.09
2001	$ 0.11
2002	$ 0.12
2003	$ 0.16
2004	$ 0.26
2005	$ 0.37
2006	$ 0.57
2007	$ 0.72
2008	$ 0.88
2009	$ 0.97

2. Rollins Inc (symbol ROL—US)

Often with investing it's the most boring, low-technology companies that offer the best returns. Rollins Inc owns Orkin Extermination, which is one of the world's largest pest control service providers. Think about it—if you have termites or other pests are you going to price compare extensively or are you going to call a company that you trust that will get rid of your problem quickly? Peter Lynch (the former star investor at the Fidelity Magellan Fund) mentioned that investors should look for companies that do something unappealing—and getting rid of cockroaches and termites seems to qualify!

This company has no debt and it has a good history of increasing profits. In addition, it operates in North America, Europe, Latin America, the Caribbean, the Middle East, and Asia—so it earns its income from many different parts of the globe. Furthermore, its growth is expected to continue. Here's a quick snapshot of its 10-year dividend history:

Year	Dividend/Share
2000	$ 0.06
2001	$ 0.06
2002	$ 0.06
2003	$ 0.09
2004	$ 0.11
2005	$ 0.13
2006	$ 0.17
2007	$ 0.20
2008	$ 0.25
2009	$ 0.28

Aside from this business offering a service people need, I like the fact that the Rollins family owns over half the stock—meaning they have a vested interest in how well the company performs. This is always reassuring for small investors because you know that they, "Eat their own cooking" (benefit based on how well the company performs).

3. Leon's Furniture (symbol LNF—Can)

I know this should be under the retail section of the book but it is a little different than the types of companies I usually like to invest in so I thought I'd put it here so it would stick out. This company sells furniture across Canada. Generally I would say selling furniture is not a great business as people buy less during economic slowdowns, furniture is not something people buy regularly like food, and retailers generally command little loyalty from customers.

However, this company is an exception. For starters, it has been in business for over 100 years—which means it has survived adversity over time. From personal experience I know that customer satisfaction is embedded in the company DNA as I have shopped at Leon's before. The salespeople operate on straight commission and it's my understanding that the delivery people also get paid with incentives. This fact was explained to me when I had a sofa delivered recently. This sort of payment arrangement motivates employees to perform. The company is very conservatively managed with no debt. In addition, it likes to own the properties from which it operates.

Let's take a moment to think about all this...The company operates in a somewhat cyclical industry. However, by linking the pay of employees to sales (using commission) the company allows costs to fall when sales fall—a sort of "shock absorber" for profits. In addition, by owning most of its stores outright (with no debt), the fixed costs are lower and the company has the ability to weather adversity.

Overall this company earns good returns on equity for shareholders and continues to rack up profits. As an interesting aside, one of its largest competitors, The Brick, was forced to cut distributions in early 2009 to preserve cash due to the difficult operating environment and declining sales. The response from Leon's...pay a special dividend *in addition to the regular dividends.*

Here's a quick look at the dividend history (note the company's special dividends paid fairly regularly):

Year	Dividend/Share
2000	$ 0.08
2001	$ 0.08
2002 *	$ 0.22
2003	$ 0.13
2004	$ 0.19
2005	$ 0.20
2006 *	$ 0.35
2007	$ 0.28
2008 *	$ 0.38
2009 *	$ 0.48
2010	(projected) $ 0.32

* Indicates special dividends paid in 2002, 2006, 2008, and 2009. The regular annual dividend has increased from $ 0.08 per share in 2000 to $0.32 per share in 2010. In addition the company has been buying back their own shares.

I have said in the past that over 95% of stocks are not worth owning at any price. Some companies have to run faster and faster on the "treadmill", competing with other companies for meagre profits. This list focuses on the elite 5% of the market and offers some investing ideas. Realize that there are other companies out there that would be great investments but this is a great starting list. I tried to include a combination of higher-yielding and lower-yielding but faster growing stocks for you.

I would like to move on and look at the prices investors pay to buy stocks in the next chapter.

CHAPTER 19

REMEMBER TO LOOK
IN THE BARGAIN BIN!

*"The market is fond of making mountains of
molehills and exaggerating ordinary vicissitudes
into major setbacks."*
—**Ben Graham**

The companies I listed operate in many different industries but they are all simple to understand. Being an
"idiot", I prefer to avoid any kinds of companies that
might confuse me (I still can't figure out *exactly* what
Nortel's business was). There are no technology stocks—
not because technology stocks can't make you rich—but
because they are too difficult for me to determine how
long into the future they will make money for investors.
If you are smarter than me, feel free to venture out and
broaden your investment horizons. But for me:

*My investing intelligence lies not in what I know—but
instead, knowing clearly what I don't know—and
avoiding that area in most cases.*

Please realize that this is a list of great companies with
bright futures. This is my investing approach. I'm a lazy
guy and prone to mistakes, so I would like to find the
highest quality companies to invest in and then tuck them
away in a drawer and let the companies earn higher
profits over time and make me wealthier in the process.

*With my investing approach, the MOST IMPORTANT
factor I look for is quality companies that have
some sort of advantage that will exist for many
years to come.*

These companies will NOT be the stocks that can
make you the most money! Stocks that can make a lot of
money over a short period of time generally involve more
risk. I'm simply not smart enough to know which of these
companies will be great investments, so I don't invest that
way. This is a list of conservative stocks that should do
pretty well without adding worry to your life.

The goal is to buy these stocks at a reasonable price.

This does not mean they are priced right for you to buy them as I am writing this. Attempting to do that with a book would be foolish as the stock prices will have changed by the time you read this. At the time of this writing, some of these companies seem cheap to me, others expensive. The main point is that this list of companies should endure and continue to increase profits (and dividends) over time—regardless of how the world unfolds going forward—but you have to buy them at reasonable prices.

How do you do that?

Buying cheaply is not an absolute science. Even the greatest investors in the world don't have an *exact* dollar amount of what stocks are worth. However, there are guidelines.

Many investors have a list of stocks they would like to buy…and then they patiently wait for the opportunity to buy them cheaply. For researching historical stock prices, I would look at *Value Line*. This is a binder containing many of the large Canadian interlisted stocks as well as major US stocks. You can find a copy of it at most major libraries. You can look up the company and see if the price is cheap compared with its history. If the price seems expensive, you can wait until an opportunity presents itself. Generally you are looking for an event or something that will allow you to buy these great companies at cheap prices. This happens from time-to-time and it offers you a chance to buy cheaply. To be honest, I've missed some great opportunities to buy stocks cheaply, but overall these opportunities come again—if you're patient. Here are some examples of a few different times stocks have become cheap...

1. TransCanada Pipelines

Back in 1999, TransCanada shares were trading for around $20/share and they paid a dividend of $1.12. This gave investors a dividend return of around 5.5%. Then in December, the company surprisingly cut its dividend to 80 cents. The plan was to preserve some capital and grow their business. This company—with it vast network of pipelines was crucial to modern life—it was not about to go bankrupt. But the stocks took a beating, falling to around $10/share within a few months. Investors who bought then were earning an 8% dividend. Today the shares are selling for around $38 each—almost quadrupling the value for investors who bought at the bottom. In addition, the dividend has risen to $1.60 per share. So investors who bought after the shares crashed are now earning 16% per year on their initial investment!

2. Colgate

I dedicated a whole chapter in my first book to this one. Back in late 2004, Colgate had a bad quarter and earnings came in under expectations and the shares dropped below $45. Investors who bought then did okay (even after the stock market setback in 2008-2009). As of this writing, the shares are trading over $80, so investors have nearly doubled their money in 6 years. Realize that stock prices are volatile, but Colgate has over 100 years of dividend-paying history with over 40 years of increases. Right now the shares are paying over $2.12 per share. So investors are now earning almost 5% in dividends if they purchased the shares when the company faced short-term trouble. And the company should keep increasing dividends for decades to come.

3. Canadian Oil Sands

One of my better investments was in 2003-2004. During this time Syncrude (a Canadian Oil Sands production jointly owned by various oil companies) was expanding production. However, the costs of these projects kept going up. With each cost overrun announcement, the stock price took a hit. At that time I was able to buy shares at around $8 each. I sold these shares in early 2009 at almost $20 each. Today the shares offer a $2 dividend—which means investors who bought when I did are earning 25% per year in dividends

These are simply a few examples of opportunities that have arisen. Good chances to buy great companies at reasonable prices do happen from time-to-time...so be ready for them. By sticking to wonderful companies like the ones I've included on the list of "idiot-proof" stocks, you should do quite well at investing over time. I've made a lot of dumb mistakes but I've still done quite well over time. If you are smarter than me, you have a great chance of doing even better... just be patient. Now let's take a look at companies life cycles so you can understand this approach a little more clearly.

CHAPTER 20

COMPANY LIFE CYCLES—
WHERE TO LOOK FOR
"IDIOT-PROOF" STOCKS

"To every thing there is a season..."
—**Ecclesiastes 3.1**

Just as people go through life cycles from infancy to adolescence and on to maturity and then old age, companies go through similar life cycles. If you want to make money through investing, it's important for you to know what stage in the life cycle your stocks are in. More importantly, at what stage is it the best to invest in companies?

1. Infancy

Infancy in people is a time for discovery and incredible learning. You start out as a totally helpless being but gradually you reach certain milestones over time. One day you're able to support your head, then you start eating food, then you sit up, you crawl, you walk, you begin to talk... However, even though you are developing very quickly, during this entire period you are *totally* dependent on care from others—you simply could not survive all on your own.

It's the same with companies. In the beginning a new company might simply be an idea. Money (and incredible effort) is invested to form the company, create products, formulate a business plan, make sales, and slowly begin to earn revenue. At this stage the company is totally dependent on the efforts and money from its founders and/or investors. It's most common for the company to be losing money at this stage and companies in their infancy are also prone to making many huge mistakes. The investors here are often sophisticated venture capitalists who take on tremendous risks (as many of these companies don't survive) with the hope of earning huge potential profits. This investing approach is pretty high risk and involves intelligence that is beyond my grasp—so I would not even try to invest in companies at this stage.

2. Fast Growth ("Adolescence")

This is the stage where the company (if it survived the first stage), really begins to grow. It has a business strategy and is acting on it. At this stage, the company might still be losing money but the future is a little clearer than during the first stage. If the company is earning a profit, it is usually reinvesting those profits back into the business. It's quite rare for companies to offer dividends to investors at this stage. Often venture capitalists will want to get their money out of the company and it will offer an initial public offering (IPO). This means that it sells shares to the public and the original investors are able to cash out. This is an area where some investors can make a lot of money if they buy the correct companies at reasonable prices. This stage can last for a number of years and often the share price for stocks at this stage is quite expensive. However just like with adolescents, huge mistakes can be made with these companies which can cause problems and even lead to bankruptcy. Once again, in spite of the possibility for large profits, I have tended to avoid companies at this stage because they involve more risk and generally don't pay dividends.

3. Maturity

Just as with people, companies that manage to survive the first two stages reach maturity at some point. In people, this is the stage where careers have been established, there's some money in the bank, and the bills get paid on time. With companies, their business is established and the company will earn regular profits. In fact at this stage even though it can continue to grow (just as people can continue to grow in many ways and they can also get promoted) the profits of the business are often greater than the amount needed to be reinvested. Many companies at this stage will pay growing dividends. For highly profitable companies there will still be excess cash left over even after paying dividends. What management does with this extra cash will ultimately determine how much money investors ultimately earn from owning stock in these companies.

Managers and CEOs of profitable companies often fritter away extra money on stupid, wealth-destroying acquisitions.

Many people like to shop and CEOs are no different. If they use extra cash to make acquisitions, they can have interesting conversations at cocktail parties and they can often add a little more swagger to their walk. This move may impoverish investors though. History is filled with countless examples of CEOs making stupid acquisitions. For example, during the 1970s Coca Cola owned Columbia Pictures along with water projects, a shrimp farm, and a winery. This was an example of a great company acquiring crummy businesses—and it cost shareholders. In the 1980s with a new CEO at the helm, Coke divested all these businesses to concentrate on its core business and profits (and dividends) exploded upwards. In Canada, BCE (the parent company of Bell Canada) was a cash cow for years but used its profits to make numerous dumb acquisitions.

Some acquisitions create wealth for investors, but most don't!

What should a company that is making bucketfuls of money (even after paying out a good dividend) do with its extra money? Share buybacks are often a good choice. Let me explain.

Suppose you think of a company's profits as a large apple pie which has to be dividend amongst shareholders. In this situation there are two ways for YOU as a shareholder to get a bigger piece of pie (a larger share of the profits). You can try to make a bigger pie (make an acquisition to earn more profit) or you can cut the pie into fewer pieces. Making a bigger and bigger pie can become cumbersome (just as acquiring new businesses to run can be difficult). It's much easier to keep making the same size pie, but divide it into larger pieces. So if you start off with 10 shareholders who are entitled to a piece of the pie, if the pie remains the same size BUT you pay a couple of shareholders to go away (the company buys back their shares), you now only have to divide the pie among eight people.

Think about it… Isn't it logical to assume that people running a certain business are the people who know the most about that particular business? Isn't it also logical to assume that the more investors know about a business the more successful they will be at investing in it? Therefore in many cases, doesn't it make sense for managers to invest in businesses they know the most about (their own company), and buy back shares.

Let's give you a real-life example to show this.

One of the companies I like (and own shares in) is Dun and Bradstreet. This is one of the companies in my "idiot-proof" list of stocks and it is definitely a mature company —founded over 150 years ago. From 2000-2009, its total revenues grew from around 1.4 billion to less than 1.7 billion. For this 10-year period, the company's revenue grew by only 19% in total or less than 2% per year.

BUT the company also does something very friendly for shareholders—it buys back its own shares. In 2000, the company had over 80 million shares outstanding whereas by 2009, there were only 51 million shares outstanding. So the company bought back over one third of all its shares in 10 years. The result is that earnings per share (the amount YOU are entitled to for each share you own) increased from $1.50/share to $5.42/share (they grew over 260%)! Even though the "pie" did not grow that much, each shareholder now receives a MUCH bigger piece!

Share buybacks can be a great (and low-risk) way for companies to give more money to shareholders!

Since most of my investments are in mature companies, I like to see regular share buybacks because it shows me that managers are interested in creating wealth for shareholders rather than simply growing their empires at any cost.

Before I go on to explain the last stage of the company life cycle, I want to add a point about mature companies. These companies can keep growing at a reasonable rate for many decades—so they are suitable investments for people who like the fact that they are established and hence are often low-risk, dividend-growers. Here's a quick excerpt from a Fortune Magazine business article that appeared discussing how Coca Cola had reached saturation and how it would be difficult for the company to keep growing:

"Several times every year a weighty and serious investor looks long and with profound respect at Coca-Cola's record, but comes regretfully to the conclusion that he is looking too late. The spectres of saturation and competition rise before him."

The article argues that Coke's days of growth are numbered. This article was written half a century after the launch of coke—in 1938. Since then case volume has grown from 200 million to over 10 billion! A $40 investment bank in 1938 would now be worth tens of thousands of dollars today! Mature companies can grow MUCH longer than people assume. This is the area I like to invest in because the risk of a company that has been operating for decades (that offer simple, recession-proof products) suddenly going out of business is low. In this area, you can benefit from reasonable growth and increasing dividends for a long, long time.

4. Decline

The sad reality of life, for both people and companies is that after maturity (which can vary in length) comes decline. It is difficult to pinpoint the exact time a company enters the decline stage. For example, GM gained market share and increased profits for decades until it entered a long decline phase. The same can be said for K-mart, Kodak, and a host of other formerly great companies.

Realize that there can be situations where some investors might point to decline while others still see measured growth. Let me give you an example of a company some investors would consider to be in decline...

Philip Morris (the maker of Marlboro cigarettes) was far and away the best-performing stock from 1957-2003 of the US large companies—making many investors a LOT OF WEALTH. But it's also true that the US tobacco market has been in volume decline for decades. For a while, Philip Morris continued to grow by stealing market share but now even with market share gains, the total volume of US cigarette sales is in decline. But the company has managed to record ever-increasing profits and increasing dividends for years longer than most people expected.

Another example of a company at this stage would be Davis and Henderson—a company in the cheque-printing business. This is an area that is definitely in decline as fewer people use cheques, but this company has been raising distributions gradually since 2001 and enriching shareholders in the process. Companies can be in decline but remain profitable for years. Many of the companies that became income trusts were companies in decline— but they paid out generous dividends.

I used a lot of these income trusts to earn a high enough income to leave the rat race as early as possible and combined them with a lot of mature companies that offered growing profits and dividends. However, now that I am earning other income, I prefer to focus on the mature companies that offer growth since its more tax-effective.

I try to avoid companies in the first two stages because although these companies *might* offer a chance for huge profits, the risks are greater. I am not smart enough to separate the ultimate winners that sizzle from the losers that fizzle. I also want to avoid companies in decline because it is difficult for me to know how quickly they will decline and how much cash I will get in the interim.

Mature companies that are still growing can offer reasonable growth for decades and combine this with dividend increases—while being relatively low-risk investments for investors over the long-term. These are the kinds of companies you find on the list of "idiot-proof" stocks.

Now let's take a quick look at how taxes affect your investment decisions.

CHAPTER 21

DEATH, TAXES, AND TRIPS TO THE DENTIST

"The tax collector must love poor people, he's creating so many of them."
—Bill Vaughan

I wish I had the power to help you avoid death and trips to the dentist—but I don't. However I can help you with a little useful information on taxes as they relate to investing. I know—hearing about taxes is about as much fun as a trip to the dentist, but I think I can offer you some thoughts that can save you some money.

Some people have gone to extreme lengths in the past to avoid paying taxes. For example, Howard Hughes moved from hotel to hotel in different states within the US (making sure he never stayed more than the recognized

180 days) in order to avoid paying state taxes. Later he sold his company shares to the Hughes Medical Institute so that they would be sheltered as a tax-exempt charity. When he died, his estate completely avoided state taxes because his "state of residence" could not be legally determined. Although few people want to go to such extreme lengths to avoid paying taxes, a little planning can make a huge difference.

First off—realize that income taxes were implemented as a "temporary" measure in 1917—so they might be repealed at any time (I don't really know how long "temporary" is). However, until they are eliminated, you have the legal right to take every legal action possible to reduce your taxes.

* Note: For most people, looking at tax rules is BORING. For me it's about as much fun as watching paint dry. So I've tried to keep it short and give you the basic information as it relates to investing. Then if you are really lazy, I've offered the key tips at the very end, so you can simply skip to the end of the chapter if you don't want to read the dry stuff. Let's get started...

When I retired at 34, one of the cornerstones of my strategy was to recognize that taxes are the single biggest expense faced by most people. By simply earning a tax-advantaged income (such as Canadian dividends), my tax bill almost vanished (while the level of services I received remained the same). By removing this huge expense, the amount I had to earn to live was much less. Here's a quick

look at the percentage tax you will pay at the top tax rate
in each province and territory (these are 2009 figures):

Province	Ordinary Income%	Capital Gains%	Eligible Dividends%
Alberta	39.00	19.50	14.55
British Columbia	43.70	21.85	19.92
Manitoba	46.40	23.20	23.83
New Brunswick	46.00	23.00	21.80
Newfoundland	44.50	22.25	22.89
NW Territories	43.05	21.53	18.25
Nova Scotia	48.25	24.13	28.35
Nunavut	40.50	20.25	22.24
Ontario	46.41	23.20	23.06
PEI	47.37	23.69	24.44
Quebec	48.22	24.11	29.69
Saskatchewan	44.00	22.00	20.35
Yukon	42.40	21.20	17.23

Notice how the tax rate for dividends and capital gains
is *much lower* than for ordinary income (such as interest
income or working income). Remember that with
working income, you also must pay CPP and EI *on top of
paying the highest tax rates at each income level!* Along
with these high compulsory payments there are many
other working-related expenses such as union/profe-

ssional dues, commuting costs, parking, dry-cleaning,... This brings us to our first point:

The absolute most expensive way to earn income is by working for it! Collecting passive dividend income allows you to keep more of your money in your own pocket.

The chart above shows the *top tax rates*. Let's take a quick look at the Ontario tax rates for 2010 (other provinces will be similar) at each income level:

Income Amount	Ordinary Income%	Capital Gains%	Eligible Dividends%
At $37,106	24.15	12.08	(3.21)
At $40,970	31.15	15.58	6.94
At $65,038	32.98	16.49	7.45
At $74,214	35.39	17.70	10.94
At $76,664	39.41	19.70	12.91
At $81,941	43.41	21.70	18.71
At $127,022	46.41	23.20	23.06

* Notice how the dividend tax rates are extremely low at lower income levels. In fact, up to an income of $37,106, the income tax rate is actually negative for dividends! This was the main reason I decided to buy some good Canadian dividend-paying stocks and live off the dividends. By doing this my tax bill essentially vanished! Combine this fact with a paid-off house and absolutely no debt and the amount you need to earn to live on is greatly reduced.

From this we can see that Canadian-based dividend income is a great way to earn income if you don't have other income because you pay a very low rate of tax at the various income levels. However, it's different if you earn other income from either a job or self-employment. In most cases if you are currently earning an income, the best option might be contributing to an RRSP. This is because you can use pre-tax dollars to contribute to your RRSP and the plan can grow tax-free. Realize that an RRSP is not *always* your best option, but it is an effective tool for deferring taxes and building wealth. So:

*There are **no tax benefits** to holding Canadian stocks inside your RRSP. Outside RRSPs, Canadian stocks get preferential tax treatment but inside these plans you should choose the best investment—ignoring taxes.*

The reason for this is simple:

You do not benefit from favourable dividend tax rates for Canadian stocks that are inside your RRSP. You simply pay tax on any money you withdraw from your RRSP regardless of how it was invested.

You should also realize that:

If you own US stocks outside your RRSP, you will have to pay a 15% withholding tax on all dividend income received. This withholding tax MAY be recoverable through a foreign tax credit.

But you should also know:

There is no withholding tax on US stock dividends held inside an RRSP.
(This is because of the Canada/US tax treaty).

* Note: If you hold **US stocks** in a **Registered Education Savings Plan (RESP)** or **Tax-Free Savings Account (TFSA)**, you still have to pay the withholding tax.

And one final point to be aware of:

The foreign content limit for RRSPs was eliminated in 2005—meaning you can have up to 100% foreign in your RRSPs.

Let's take these rules and highlight the key points:

Key Points

1. If you are working and earning an income and want to accumulate wealth, in many cases an RRSP will be your best option.

2. If you do contribute to an RRSP, then it does not matter which kinds of companies you invest in (US or Canadian) because they are all taxed the same.
3. If you contribute to an RESP or TFSA, then you will have to pay the US withholding tax of 15% on all US dividend income.
4. If you have both an RRSP and a TFSA, it might be a good idea to hold US stocks in your RRSP and Canadian stocks in your TFSA
5. If you decide it's better to buy stocks outside of these plans, Canadian dividend stocks received favourable tax treatment. With US stocks, you will pay a 15% withholding tax, but some or all of this tax may be recoverable through a foreign tax credit.

* Note: This is not meant to be a tax guide, so I will not go any further. Realize I am not an accountant by profession—just a regular guy. For more detailed information, see an accountant or pick up a copy of "Your Personal Tax Planning Guide". You can get this booklet (which is printed by the CGAs of Ontario) for FREE from most major libraries every year around tax time.

WALK...
BEFORE YOU RUN!

"The tragedy in life doesn't lie in not reaching your goal. The tragedy lies in having no goal to reach."
—Benjamin Mays

Have you ever known someone who decides on an almost impossible goal and then starts taking action to attain that goal only to give up a short while later—such as quitting smoking *immediately* or training to run a marathon after spending decades on the couch in front of the TV. New Year's resolutions are made annually and most of them are abandoned before the winter snow has melted. Is it the same with investing?

A while ago I was giving a talk at the University of Ottawa and I was explaining how I retired in my 30s and how virtually any one of the students could invest to become wealthy while they were still young. Afterwards, a student came up and asked some questions about my talk. He mentioned that although the strategy of buying dividend-paying stocks seemed like a good way to create a passive income, the idea of living off of dividends seemed like too lofty a goal to attain.

We talked a bit more about the whole strategy, then I hit upon an idea—let's break the whole thing down into bite-sized attainable goals. If you have a goal, it becomes much easier to realize if you can claim a number of small victories instead of only focusing on "winning the war".

I noticed that virtually all the students had a cell phone and I asked him how much he spent on his plan. It cost him around $40 per month.

Okay, so $40 × 12 months plus taxes would equal about $500 per year. If he used the cell phone for his whole life at that rate, it would cost him tens of thousands of dollars. With inflation over time, it's difficult to come up with exact figures, but he would possibly spend $100,000 over his lifetime merely to use a cell phone and text his friends. That $100,000 would simply disappear into a "financial black hole" never to be seen again.

Now suppose he could save around $9,000 and invest it in the shares of his cell phone provider, which happened to be BCE (parent of Bell Mobility). At that time, the dividend yield on these shares was around 5.6%. So look at this:

$$\$9,000 \times 5.6\% = \$504$$

Note: The dividends earned would be equal to his annual cell phone bill.

By simply investing $9,000 in the shares of the company that provided his cell phone service, this student could have FREE cell phone service for the rest of his life!

Think about it...over time the cost of cell phone services will probably go up, but as they do, cell phone service providers will earn more profits and be able to increase their dividends. So as his costs go up, so would his dividends.

So the end result would be that instead of $100,000 vanishing into a "financial black hole" over time, he could instead invest around $9,000 now and *never have to pay for his cell phone service again—his dividends would pay that bill for him!* In addition, at the end instead of having nothing but bills that had been paid, the shares he invested in would probably be worth a small fortune.

This would be his first financial "victory". Next he could buy shares in an oil company such that the gas for his car would be paid by his oil company dividends. The next step might be his home heating bill by buying shares of Enbridge. After each "victory", one more bill would "disappear" forever. As the bills kept disappearing, he would get positive reinforcement to keep going until ALL his bills were paid by his dividends. And the rising costs of the bills would be offset by dividend increases.

A reader of my first book emailed telling me this was how he was using my dividend investing strategy. I have since lost the e-mail, but regardless, it is a great approach to take to gradually build wealth and stop working. You can use many of the companies on the list of "idiot-proof" stocks to accomplish this over time.

I Screwed Up!
Confessions of an Idiot

"I'm not a complete idiot. Some parts are missing"
—**Unknown**

It's early March 2009 and I am speaking with two business reporters—John Heinzl (*Globe and Mail*) and Ellen Roseman (Toronto Star). The stock market had undergone a massive bear market and I had sold my stocks a month or so prior to the conversation. I explain my reasons but the reporters' question why I would abandon my strategy of buying and holding dividend stocks forever. Even though the move has saved me tens of thousands of dollars to that point, the idea of tinkering with a strategy that allowed me to wave goodbye to the rat race at the age of 34 seems like a dumb idea. I know both of these journalists pretty well and I know from experience that they will ask me for verification of what I am saying. They often remind me of auditors with their requests for detailed documentation, but I give them what they need and they each write an article about my decision. I have wanted to shift my stock holdings to higher-growing, lower-yielding companies for a while... but now I was convinced that I could cash out of the stock market and get back in at cheaper prices at a later time. In effect, I was trying to time the market—something *nobody* has ever done consistently.

What was I thinking? What was I drinking?

Was I joking? What was I smoking?

A few months later, the stock markets had recovered somewhat. I am speaking with James Daw, another business reporter with the Toronto Star. While the other two reporters remind me of auditors looking at details, James reminds me more of a hostile lawyer cross-examining me. He questions everything quite bluntly and finally sums up the entire episode of me selling my stocks and trying to re-enter the stock market at a more opportune time with four words:

"You were an idiot!"

I didn't like hearing those words. I mean who wants to be called an idiot? But sometimes the truth hurts.

The results of my overconfidence masquerading as wisdom are included in the final chapter, "My Portfolio Update".

My Portfolio Update

> *"If you are a know-something investor, able to understand business economics and to find five to ten sensibly priced companies that possess important long-term competitive advantages, conventional diversification (broadly based active portfolios) makes no sense to you."*
> **—Warren Buffett**

I get regular emails from readers asking me various questions, but the most common request I get is to share what I have been doing with my own portfolio—which I will update here. However, if you are interested in getting more information regularly, you can join my free monthly newsletter. There is a brief explanation of how to sign up at the back of this book. (or go to www.stopworking.ca)

Originally when I wrote my first book, I had created a portfolio that was meant to allow me to leave the rat race—so it contained a lot of higher-paying dividend stocks and income trusts. But since I am now earning an income from writing and public speaking, it makes much more sense (tax-wise) to own companies that pay out smaller dividends but also grow their dividends over time. So I now prefer higher growing dividend-payers—and my portfolio choices reflect this.

* Note: As of this writing, the Canadian dollar is trading pretty close to parity with the US dollar. In addition, the US stock market has been a miserable place to invest since 2000. These factors have made US stocks relatively cheap for Canadians—so a large portion of my portfolio is in US stocks. I have tried to focus mostly on companies that earn a good portion of their earnings outside North America so that I am protected from problems specific to the US while I can also take part in the growth of many emerging markets around the world:

Canadian Stocks

Husky Energy

Imperial Oil

Manulife

Shoppers Drug Mart

Telus

US Stocks

CR Bard

Berkshire Hathaway

China Mobile

Coca Cola

Dun and Bradstreet

ExxonMobil

Flowers Foods

Johnson and Johnson

Kraft

Monsanto

Philip Morris Intl

Sysco

Wal-Mart

From a look at my current holdings, you can see that I have many of the "idiot-proof" stocks on my list in my own portfolio. However, there are some that are not on the list. A reasonable question would be "Why"? So let's go through the exceptions: Husky, Manulife, Berkshire Hathaway, China Mobile, Flowers Foods, and Monsanto

Husky Energy

This is one of Canada's largest energy companies with oil and gas production, refining, and retail operations. It is similar in many respects to Imperial Oil but Imperial is somewhat better managed. However, even though I would like exposure to the integrated oil and gas companies, I don't want too large a portion of my portfolio in one company—so I wanted to invest in a different integrated oil company. In addition, Husky has made a number of large gas discoveries in the South China sea—which is an area of the world that will be extremely thirsty for energy in the decades to come. It pays a decent dividend and should grow the dividend over time. Overall

I think Imperial Oil is the better long-term investment, but Husky is pretty good and I prefer to not have all my eggs in one basket.

Manulife

This is the largest life insurance company in Canada with numerous international operations. It has come into difficulty lately because it offered guaranteed returns based on the performance of the stock market. Many investors would consider this stock conservative, but I feel it is one of my riskier holdings because it's impossible for me to fully understand all the risks on their balance sheet. As a result, this company makes up a pretty small portion of my portfolio. However, Manulife has a history of operating in Asia (including China) and this is a fast-growing market in the world. With recent troubles some of its competitors have faced (especially AIG in the US); Manulife should be well-positioned moving forward to take business from their rivals.

Berkshire Hathaway (Warren Buffett's company)

This company would absolutely be on the "idiot-proof" list in a heartbeat if it paid dividends (one of the criteria I look for) because it is a great company. In most cases, I would never buy a stock that does not pay dividends because it's very difficult to trust that management will not squander the cash of the company on some wealth-destroying acquisition. However, Berkshire is essentially a mutual fund without any fees—run by one of the best management teams in the world. With this investment, you get the world's best investor managing money on your behalf along with ownership of many great companies which Berkshire owns.

The downside is that Buffett turned 80 in 2010, so you have to be confident that management will continue to perform well after Buffett is gone (something that Buffett has seemed determined to embed in the company's DNA). But the upside is that it controls conservatively managed insurance operations which provides Buffett with low-cost cash, which he invests. If you compare the growth of Berkshire's book value (which approximates what investors have earned) with the performance of the US stock market in general, here's what you come up with:

> (Overall Gains % from 1964-2009):
> US Stock Market (S&P 500)   = 5,430%
> Berkshire Hathaway   = 434,057%

Over this time frame, Berkshire has created more that 80 times as much wealth for investors! This *massive* outperformance will diminish because this is a large company today, but it should still outperform for many years to come...

China Mobile

This would absolutely be on my "idiot-proof" list of stocks if I actually lived where this company operated. However, I always prefer investing in companies that I can see operate regularly but I don't live in China. So why did I buy it? For starters, this company is the world's largest wireless company with over half a billion subscribers— and wireless companies tend to earn good profits. It commands a 60% market share in China and an even higher share in rural China (the area of future growth). Its finances are rock solid with only $5 billion in debt BUT over $47 billion in cash. I bought the shares because they were cheap and the company offers a product that generates pretty stable profits (people pay their cell phone bills every month). In addition, the Chinese Yuan should gradually rise *over the longer term* which will be a boon to foreign investors.

Flowers Foods

Founded in 1919, this company has the largest dollar value market share of fresh packaged breads (22.9%) compared to its competitor, Sara Lee (8.4%). It has managed to grow earnings per share at over 20% per year since 2005 (although growth will be slower in the future). It has increased dividends from a meagre 1 cent per share in 2002 to an annualized rate of 80 cents as of this writing.

The company offers products everyone needs (baked food) and should be recession-proof. The main reason it did not make my list is that it offers products that don't have the same brand loyalty as the other companies on the "idiot-proof" list. I bought the shares because they were cheap, with a good track record of growth and better operating numbers than their competitors.

Monsanto

The world population is expected to grow from around 6.5 billion today to around 9 billion by 2050. In addition, many people in the world are becoming wealthier and demanding richer diets—which means a lot more food will have to be produced on smaller amounts of land. Monsanto is the largest player in genetic engineering providing the technology in 90% of the worlds genetically engineered seeds. This technology has created tremendous controversy but it has also benefitted in the growing of various crops. This is a company that I would never include on my "idiot-proof" list of companies because it relies on patents that do expire and it is difficult to determine the future. However, I have a small portion of my portfolio in this company because in spite of possible risks, it dominates its market and has huge growth potential. In addition, its patents are different than those of pharmaceutical companies. With drug companies, as soon as patents expire, consumers can buy the generic equivalent. Monsanto on the other hand licenses its seed technology to its competitors so new biotech innovations must be designed to work with Monsanto's technology. This dominance has made the company the target of an antitrust inquiry—just as Microsoft faced a few years ago. Income has increased quickly over the last decade and dividends have risen more than 4-fold during that same timeframe.

Realize that all these companies are good quality stocks that I am happy to own shares in. However, each of them had one or two small issues which prevented me from including them on my list of "idiot-proof" stocks.

The Results of Exiting the Stock Market in Early 2009...

As I mentioned earlier, I stupidly sold my stocks in 2009 hoping to buy them back more cheaply. During this time I followed the strategy outlined in my third book, *Money for Nothing* and sold put options on stocks I wanted to pick up cheaply—hoping to buy them. Here's a list of some of the stocks I sold (and later bought back). I have used Canadian dollar prices because after I sold my stocks I kept my money in our currency because I didn't trust what was happening in the US:

Stock	Price Sold	Price Bought Back	Gain/Loss
Husky Energy	$ 29.31	$ 30.66	–$ 1.35
Manulife	$ 22.18	$ 21.95	$ 0.23
Johnson and Johnson	$ 72.67	$ 63.56	$ 9.11
Wal-Mart	$ 57.75	$ 54.20	$ 3.55
Philip Morris	$ 52.49	$ 52.67	–$ 0.16

And here's a list of the new companies I purchased. I have included the prices they were at when I sold my entire portfolio back in early February 2009, and the prices I bought them back for eventually—to show the difference waiting for the stocks made:

Stock	Price (Feb 2009)	Price Bought	Gain/(Loss)
CR Bard	$ 86.60	$ 79.10	$ 7.50
Imperial Oil	$ 40.04	$ 40.71	–$ 0.67
* Berkshire Hathaway	$ 58.00	$ 75.80	–$ 17.80
China Mobile	$ 73.60	$ 47.86	$ 25.74
Shoppers Drug Mart	$ 50.70	$ 38.00	$ 12.70
Coca Cola	$ 59.25	$ 53.67	$ 5.58
Telus	$ 42.07	$ 34.05	$ 8.02
Dun and Bradstreet	$ 88.40	$ 73.28	$ 15.12
ExxonMobil	$ 81.71	$ 69.93	$ 11.78
Flowers Foods	$ 24.37	$ 22.35	$ 2.02

Kraft	$ 28.81	$ 26.96	$ 1.85
Monsanto	$109.92	$ 71.74	$ 38.18
Sysco	$ 29.24	$ 27.98	$ 1.26

* Berkshire Hathaway is adjusted for a 50-1 stock split as a result of the Burling Northern acquisition

From a quick glance at the charts, it seems that I did well by exiting the market and re-entering later. But I don't want to give the wrong impression—there were some factors that helped me:

1. I was able to pocket option premiums which earned me money.
2. The Canadian dollar rose massively against the US dollar.
3. I only reinvested my cash in companies that were cheap—but some of the companies I might have liked to buy had run up in price so that I was not able to buy them.

In addition, I did not see the whole stock market crash coming—but to be fair, neither did most investors. Even Buffett lost billions on an oil company's shares, Conoco-Phillips, which he bought slightly before the crash. But he made up for any mistakes he made before the crash by making many savvy moves afterwards. I didn't. That's the reason Warren Buffett is a genius multi-billionaire and I am an idiot millionaire.

Also realize that this exercise of selling during the market turmoil was not worth the effort. It was stressful trying to buy stocks at the right price. Overall, I would have been better off to change my portfolio to higher-growing companies *gradually* rather than trying to guess the movements of the market and doing it all at once. But I guess—stupid is as stupid does. Live and learn I suppose. Now on to you...

The easy secret to amassing wealth is to buy "idiot-proof" stocks and let them make you wealthy over time. This is NOT complicated. This book shows you how to do that—even if you are not an expert investor. It even provides you with a list to start with.

Now...you are at a very important fork in the road of life. Will you decide to keep on the same path you have been travelling on? How has that worked out for you so far? I decided to veer off and do things differently...and for me that has made all the difference. Which path will you choose?

Looking for a Speaker For Your Next Event?

Are you looking for a dynamic speaker who is the exact opposite of the stereotypical dry financial speaker? Do you want someone who combines humour and personal stories that capture the attention of your audience?

Derek Foster offers a down-to-earth approach in explaining simple investing concepts that allowed him to become a millionaire and leave the rat race by the time he was 34! He has also written numerous National Bestselling investment books explaining his approach.

He is a highly sought after speaker and has captured the attention of various audiences. TV experiences include interviews on Breakfast Television, CBC "The Hour", ROBTV, and CTV Newsnet along with many others. Derek has also given live presentations across Canada in front of many diverse audiences.

To bring financial speaker Derek Foster to your next event, contact us:

Foster Underhill Financial Press
900 Greenbank Road, Suite 508, Ottawa, ON K2J 4P6
Telephone: **(613) 823-2143**   Toll-free: **1-888-686-7867**
www.stopworking.ca

FREE E-letter

Sign up for my free e-letter (it takes seconds to join):

Go to: www.stopworking.ca
Click on: "Free Newsletter" (left side of the page)
Scroll down to the bottom of the page
Click on: The "Click Here" box

Enter your email address, click send, and you're done!

* This service is free and I do not sell or give your email address to any third parties. This is simply a way for me to stay connected with you and keep you updated on investment events as they happen.

Recommended Reading List

STOP WORKING: Here's How You Can!
Derek Foster

The Lazy Investor
Derek Foster

Money for Nothing and Your Stocks for Free (advanced investors)
Derek Foster

STOP WORKING TOO: You Still Can!
Derek Foster

One Up on Wall Street
Peter Lynch

Beating The Street
Peter Lynch

The Future For Investors
Jeremy Siegel

Stocks For the Long Run
Jeremy Siegel

The Warren Buffett Way
Robert Hagstrom

The Ultimate Dividend Playbook
Josh Peters

Dividends Still Don't Lie
Kelley Wright

The Snowball: Warren Buffett and the Business of Life
Alice Schroeder

The Little Book of Big Dividends
Charles Carlson